# Getting to Know...

# CARS & MOTORING

## ...an introduction for the younger enthusiast

### Edited by Derek Sansom

Published by Panda Publishing, Manchester and London.
Distributed by Jupiter Books, 167 Hermitage Road,
    London, N4 (01-800 6601).
Origination by Harry Darton & Associates Ltd, London.
Printed by Chapel River Press, Andover, Hants.
© 1974 Panda Publishing. SBN 85688 010 8.

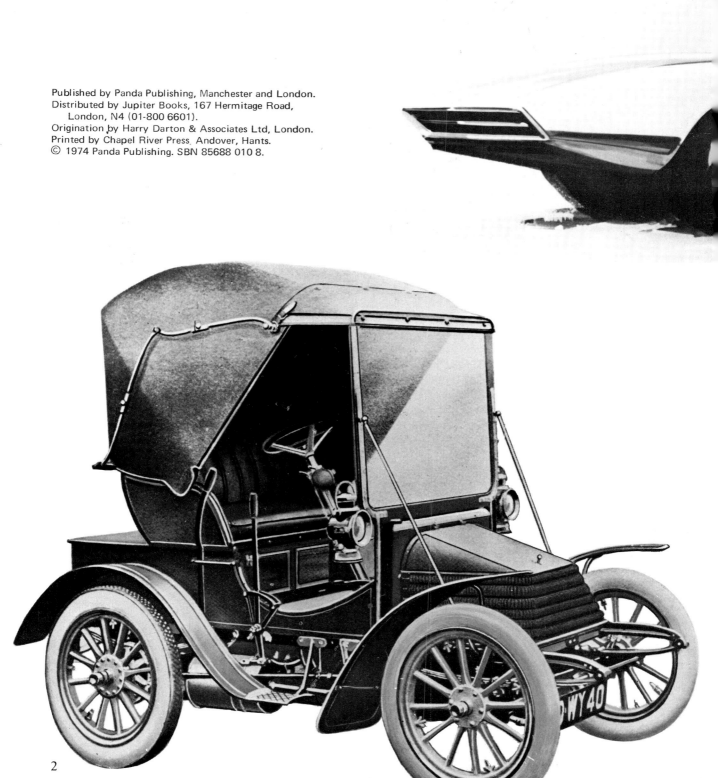

# CONTENTS

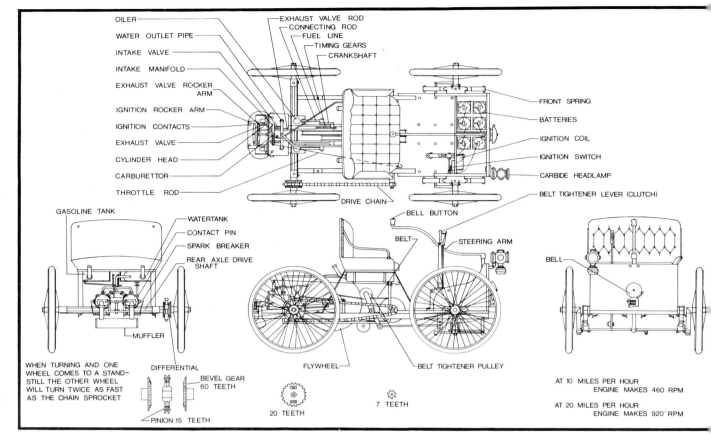

OILER
WATER OUTLET PIPE
INTAKE VALVE
INTAKE MANIFOLD
EXHAUST VALVE ROCKER ARM
IGNITION ROCKER ARM
IGNITION CONTACTS
EXHAUST VALVE
CYLINDER HEAD
CARBURETTOR
THROTTLE ROD

EXHAUST VALVE ROD
CONNECTING ROD
FUEL LINE
TIMING GEARS
CRANKSHAFT

FRONT SPRING
BATTERIES
IGNITION COIL
IGNITION SWITCH
CARBIDE HEADLAMP
BELT TIGHTENER LEVER (CLUTCH)

DRIVE CHAIN

GASOLINE TANK
WATERTANK
CONTACT PIN
SPARK BREAKER
REAR AXLE DRIVE SHAFT

BELL BUTTON
BELT
STEERING ARM
BELL

MUFFLER

WHEN TURNING AND ONE WHEEL COMES TO A STAND-STILL THE OTHER WHEEL WILL TURN TWICE AS FAST AS THE CHAIN SPROCKET

DIFFERENTIAL
BEVEL GEAR 60 TEETH

PINION 15 TEETH

20 TEETH

7 TEETH

FLYWHEEL
BELT TIGHTENER PULLEY

AT 10 MILES PER HOUR ENGINE MAKES 460 RPM
AT 20 MILES PER HOUR ENGINE MAKES 920 RPM

## Getting to know . . .
# MILESTONES of MOTORING

THE HISTORY OF the motor car as we know it today really starts with the invention of the internal combustion engine more than 100 years ago. Its development, however, owes a great deal to the steam-propelled coaches which were operating scheduled public services in Britain during the early part of the nineteenth century.

*1801* saw Britain's first steam carriage built by Cornishman, Richard Trevithick.

*1830* A steam car built by Ogle and Summers reached a top speed of 35mph. During the next decade, steam coaches were used widely throughout Britain, and a number of public services were operated between main towns.

*1865* The Locomotives Act imposed at 4mph speed limit (2mph in towns) and required a crew of three for all mechanically propelled vehicles, stipulating that one

of the crew must walk not less than 60 yards in front carrying a red flag by day and a lantern by night.

*1876* Nikolaus Otto's four-stroke engine was under development in Germany.

*1978* The requirement to carry a red flag in front of a mechanically propelled vehicle was abolished, but a crew member still had to walk in front to warn horsemen — at a reduced distance of 20 yards.

*1885* The first practical petrol-burning motor car was built by Carl Benz, a German. A fellow countryman, Gottlieb Daimler, installed a four-stroke engine in the wooden frame of a "boneshaker" to produce the world's first motor cycle.

*1888* James Boyd Dunlop, a Scottish veterinary surgeon, invented the pneumatic tyre; it was first used on bicycles.

*1894* Probably the first petrol-engined car imported into Britain was brought over from France. A four

Henry Ford's first "car" — the Quadricycle of 1896 (drawings of the Quadricycle appear on page four).

were enforced by the police with unreasonable severity; speed traps were set up, and drivers were prosecuted for having number-plates and rear lights obscured by even a light covering of mud — almost inevitable after a few miles travel on the poor roads of the period. Local magistrates were often drawn from the ranks of horse-loving gentry, and convictions and heavy fines were frequently imposed after the flimsiest of evidence.

*1905* The Automobile Association was founded in June. Its first secretary, Mr. Stenson Cooke, worked from a small office at 18 Fleet Street, London. A number of enthusiasts had banded together and, at weekends, hired the services of a handful of cyclists — most of whom were employed as Fleet Street messengers. Their job was to patrol the Surrey roads to locate police speed traps and warn motorists.

1905 — a band of enthusiasts employ speed-trap "Scouts".

horse-power Panhard, it was purchased by the Hon. Evelyn Ellis.

*1896* Henry Ford built his first car in the USA (above, pages 4 and 5). In Britain, the law requiring someone to walk in front of a vehicle was abolished, and speeds of up to 12mph were allowed. To celebrate this, the newly-formed Motor Car Club organised an Emancipation Run from London to Brighton — an event still commemorated annually. The manufacture of Daimler cars was begun in Coventry, and the Prince of Wales (later Edward VII) had his first car ride.

*1897* The Royal Automobile Club was founded.

*1902* Frederick Simms founded the Society of Motor Manufacturers and Traders (SMMT).

*1904* The Motor Car Act, raising the speed limit from 12 to 20mph, came into force. There were then 8,465 private cars, 5,345 "hackneys" and some 4,000 goods vehicles in use in Britain. Driving licences and registration plates were introduced. The new regulations

The early AA patrols wore armbands and large discs on their chests. The "all clear" side was white, but when the red side was showing a passing motorist would know that a police trap lay ahead on the road.

*1910* The first road tax, known as the Road Fund Licence, was introduced and petrol tax was fixed at threepence a gallon.

*1912* The AA published its first foreign touring guide, started its hotel classification and installed the first of its many roadside telephone boxes.

*1919* The Ministry of Transport was first established. The first post-war Motor Show was held, and a gallon of petrol cost four shillings.

*1923* Britain's motor vehicle population passed the one million mark. People were becoming more accident and road safety conscious, and the Royal Society for the Prevention of Accidents was born.

*1930* The Road Traffic Act abolished the 20mph speed limit, introduced compulsory third-party insurance and stringent provisions for dealing with careless and dangerous driving. Provision was also made for a Highway Code.

*1933* More than 2,250,000 vehicles were in use on Britain's roads, about half of them cars. The AA enrolled its 500,000th member, and its secretary Stenson Cooke was knighted.

*1934* Mr Leslie Hore-Belisha, after whom pedestrian crossing Belisha beacons were later named, started his four-year term as Minister of Transport. A new Road Traffic Act — largely concerned with road safety — imposed a 30mph speed limit in built-up areas, introduced driving tests and stiffened the penalties for reckless and dangerous driving.

*1939* Shortly before war broke out, John Cobb set up a new world land-speed record of 369.7mph. The war hit motoring hard and petrol rationing was introduced. AA membership slumped from 725,000 to 316,000.

*1945* The Motor Industry Research Association was formed to provide car manufacturers with co-operative facilities for research and testing.

*1946* The SMMT celebrated the 50th Jubilee of the birth of the motor industry with a cavalcade of nearly 500 motor vehicles reviewed by King George VI. The AA campaigned for the use of bombed sites as car parks and introduced its free breakdown service. The Motor Insurers' Bureau was formed to take care of the cases where injured third parties were unable to recover damages from motorists who were unable to pay.

*1948* A flat rate tax of £10 was imposed on all cars. Mr. Alec Issigonis's Morris Minor first appeared.

*1950* Princess Anne became the AA's one millionth member on the day she was born. Petrol rationing was finally abolished. Tubeless tyres were perfected in the USA.

*1952* The British Motor Corporation was born from a union between the Austin Motor Co. and the Nuffield Organisation, merging five famous makes of car under one banner: Austin, Morris, MG, Wolseley and Riley.

*1955* Britain's first Highway Code was published. The AA Jubilee Year was celebrated under the presidency of the Duke of Edinburgh.

*1956* The Road Traffic Act, 1956, introduced drastic measures to promote road safety, including a compulsory annual test for vehicles ten years old or more. Parking meter schemes were discussed and the penalties for dangerous driving were increased. During the Suez crisis, petrol tax was raised from 2s 6d to 3s 6d a gallon. The Institute of Advanced Motorists was formed to encourage motorists to take a pride in their driving.

*1958* Britain's first stretch of motorway — the 8½-mile Preston By-pass — was opened on 5th December. Parking meters were installed in Mayfair, London.

*1959* BMC launched the Mini, designed by Issigonis. The first 72 miles of the M1 were opened.

*1960* New legislation provided for the appointment of traffic wardens by the police and the introduction of the fixed-penalty system under which motorists would be given the opportunity in certain cases to pay a fixed fine to avoid prosecution.

Fund Tax) was increased to £17 10s. The total number of vehicles in use in Britain was just short of 13,000,000, threequarters of them cars. Road casualties reached an all-time peak, with 8,000 people killed and 390,000 injured on the roads during the year.

*1966* The USA adopts legislation to establish car safety standards.

*1967* The Breathalyser is introduced by the Road Traffic Act, giving police the power to stop motorists in certain circumstances and submit them to either a breath test or a blood or urine test to establish the level of alcohol in the blood.

*1968* New tyre regulations introduced in April lay down a minimum tread depth limit of 1mm for all tyres fitted to a car as well as making it illegal to have wrongly inflated or damaged tyres, or a wrong mix of tyres fitted to a car. Heavy goods vehicle tests were introduced.

*1971* The first 1,000 miles of motorway in Britain completed. New regulations introduced raising the minimum age for driving a motorcycle or motor scooter from 16 to 17 years.

*1972* Compulsory passenger insurance introduced for all vehicles. The number of vehicles on the roads in Britain passes the 15½ million mark, nearly 70 for every mile of road.

*1973* The Dutch Government ban motoring on Sunday, November 4th, as a measure to conserve petrol and oil following supply cuts from the Middle East. Belgium, Germany, Denmark and Italy follow suit. British Government set speed limit of 50mph. Ration-books ready for distribution. Chrysler (UK) switch production to small cars — eg Imps.

*1963* AA membership passed the 3,000,000 mark. The Worboys Committee, set up to examine the whole question of road signposting in Britain, recommended the adoption of a new range of road signs similar to those in use in some continental countries.

*1965* BMC built the millionth Mini and the AA celebrated its Diamond Jubilee after sixty years. The annual Vehicle Excise Licence (replacing the old Road

... A 1974 model Jaguar XJ12C

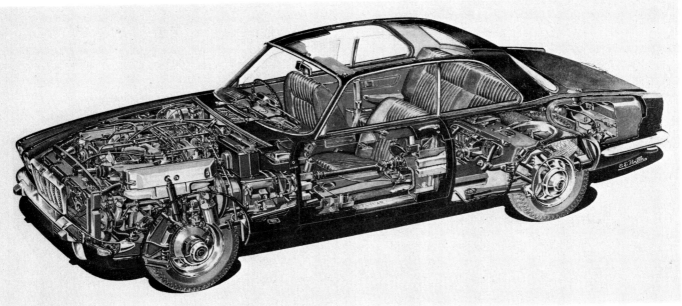

## National Motor Museum and Transport Library (Montague Motor Museum)
### Beaulieu, Brockenhurst, Hampshire.

The present Lord Montague of Beaulieu founded the Montague Motor Museum in 1952 as a memorial to his father, who was one of Britain's leading automotive pioneers. At first it consisted of a few vehicles only, displayed inside Palace House. Outbuildings were erected in 1956, when a couple of dozen cars could be seen; but within three years, a complex of new buildings housed about a hundred cars, the same amount of motor cycles and a number of commercial vehicles, bicycles, tricycles, horsedrawn vehicles, engines, models and components. Including as it does a great many extremely important exhibits on loan from other collections, the Museum is not only the largest but also the most significant in Britain.

The competition cars shown include 6C 1500 and 8C 2300 Alfa Romeos; 1908 Grand Prix and 1936 twin ohc supercharged Austins; a 1957 BRM; the famous ERA 'Romulus'; the 1907 Coppa della Velocita Itala; a W196 Mercedes-Benz of 1954; a 1936 Riley works team car; a 1908 Tourist Trophy Thronycroft; and no fewer than three holders of the World's Land Speed Record — the 1920 350hp Sunbeam, the 1000hp of 1927 from the same maker, and Sir Henry Segrave's 'Golden Arrow' of 1929. Less exciting, perhaps, but all rare, odd or exotic in some way are the 1935 Auburn speedster, 1925 19/70 Austro-Daimler, a twin-cylinder Benz of 1898, 1904 Brushmobil, Type 30 Bugatti of 1925, the 1901 Columbia electric supplied to Queen Alexandra, the elegant German Daimler of 1898, a fine 1903 De Dietrich, an Alfonso-model Hispano-Suiza, one of Field-Marshal Montgomery's Humber staff cars, the 1895 Knight (one of Britain's first cars), two Lanchesters of 1908 and 1912, the first Wolsley of 1895, a 1903 60hp Mercedes, and an extreme accentricity in the form of the 1896 Pennington.

## The Science Museum
### South, Kensington, London SW7.

The Road Transport Collection of the Science Museum is Britain's most important state transport museum. Since, as might be expected, it owns most of the more significant survivors from the early days of the British motor industry. Some of these are on loan to other museums. However among the cars to be seen at South Kensington are the second Lanchester, made in 1896; the oldest surviving Rolls-Royce (1904) and one of the first Silver Ghosts (1909); and the Rover gas turbine car of 1954 (the world's first). The collection sets out to show the history of the world's transport.

# MOTOR MUSEUMS

THE GROWING interest in old cars, trams, buses and other forms of road transport has led to the formation of several collections in various places in Britain. Among those worth visiting are:

---

### The Shuttleworth Collection
### Old Warden Aerodrome, Biggleswade, Bedfordshire

The Shuttleworth Trust was founded in memory of Richard Shuttleworth, who was killed in the Second World War and was a collector of early aircraft and cars. Cars on show in the hangars include an 1897 Daimler, 1898 Panhard-Levassor, 1898 Benz, 1899 Mors, 1900 Marot-Gardon quadricycle, 1901 Arrol-Johnston, 1901 Locomobile steamer, 1902 Bebe Peugeot, 1903 De Dietrich (probably the star of the collection), 1912 Crossley, 1913 Morris Oxford, and 1929 Alfa Romeo.

### Transport Museum
### High Street, Kingston-upon-Hull, Yorkshire.

The Transport Museum at Hull covers every form of road vehicle from manual fire engines, sleighs and sedan chairs to horsedrawn carriages and coaches (an extremely fine collection), bicycles, motor cycles, tramcars and motor cars.

### Museum of Science and Industry
### Newhall Street, Birmingham 3, Warwickshire.

The Transport Section houses about 30 cars of a remarkable range of rarity and noteworthiness, concentrating on Birmingham products. To be seen here are the monster Railton Mobil Special that held the World's Land Speed Record from 1947 to 1964, and a 200hp 'Blitzen'-type Benz of 1912. There are also a number of motor cycles.

### Myreton Motor Museum
### Near Aberlady, East Lothian.

The 35 cars in this Scottish collection include a 1924 Alvis, a Phantom 1 Rolls Royce, a very early Three Litre Bentley and a 1930 Speed Six and 1931 Eight Litre of the same make, 1930 Delage, 1927 Darracq and Galloway, several MGs, two Lagondas, a British Salmson, and a Citroen Kegresse half-track. There are a number of motor cycles and bicycles.

### Cheddar Motor Museum
### Cheddar, Somerset.

Most of the cars in the Cheddar Motor Museum are owned by members of the Veteran Car Club of Great Britain, including many of the more interesting ones.

### Trentham Motor Museum
### Trentham Gardens, Stoke-on-Trent, Staffordshire.

This collection includes cars dating from between 1899 and the 1930s, four fire engines, horsedrawn vehicles, bicycles and weapons.

### Herbert Art Gallery & Museum
### Jordan Well, Coventry, Warwickshire.

This important car collection is very much a local one, restricted to products of the Coventry area, which was the heart of the British road transport industry from the days of the first bicycles.

### Manx Motor Museum
### Crosby, Isle of Man

This collection of 20 to 30 vehicles, horsedrawn and mechanically propelled, which ranges over the century 1850-1950, starts chronologically with a horsedrawn fire engine and ends with cars that include several Bentleys of the 1920s.

### Murray's Motor Cycle Museum
### The Bungalow, Snaefell, Isle of Man.

Murray's Motor Cycle Museum, situated on the Tourist Trophy course, contains upwards of 130 machines dating from between 1901 and 1940.

### Museum of Transport
### 25 Albert Drive, Glasgow.

In addition to cars, the Glasgow Museum of Transport contains collections of tramcars, bicycles, horsedrawn vehicles, locomotives and models. The motor vehicles number between 20 and 30, of which well over half are of Scottish origin.

### The Doune Collection
### Doune Park, Doune, Perthshire.

Lord Doune's private collection. The most interesting are undoubtedly the 1929 and 1934 Maserati Grand Prix cars (the latter being ex-Whitney Straight and Prince Bira); and two Hispano-Suizas, one an H6B of 1924 and the other an unusual Type 26 of 1934, with 4½-litre Ballot engine.

### Veteran and Vintage Car Museum
### Caister Castle, Great Yarmouth.

There are over 50 cars in this collection, as well as motor cycles.

# Getting to know . . .

# How a car is created

THE MAJORITY of us take cars so much for granted that we forget – perhaps have not even enquired – how much hard work and manpower, to say nothing of investment, goes into their production. It is difficult to appreciate how much initial planning is involved, how research and testing procedures are carried out, and how many man-hours eventually go into the creation of the cars we see on our roads every day.

The early days of the motor "industry" were certainly a far cry from the vast resources involved today. From these humble beginnings, however, have emerged huge production facilities backed up by departments unthought of by the dynamic personalities to whom we owe our present motor industries. The early men involved in car building (which seems a word far more apt to the then "cottage industry") were individuals who had to rely on their own or their partner's inventive genius, dynamic character, or creative talents in order to survive if not succeed.

Instead of huge departments, each carrying out specific functions related to a new model's design, we would have seen one or possibly a small group whose job it was to create each and every item concerned. It might also befall this one man or the small team to take charge of final production needs, even the marketing strategy!

Technology has grown apace since the early days of the motor industry — and we are talking in terms of only 60 and 70 years ago — when the most important item of the car was the engine. Around this grew the rest of the vehicle! Hopefully, it would have good characteristics and look appealing enough to satisfy the

A new design gets the clay treatment. Special templates check for accuracy once the "pudding" is smoothed off. A measuring bridge can be seen in the background.

ever-increasing demand for motorised transport. Perhaps it would also make the firm a profit? In many cases it did not, and from a myriad car-building industry grew several combines and associations which eventually adopted a single identity despite the individualities in their make-up.

The pioneering days are gone to a large extent – though there are still pockets of ingenious design and futuristic concepts. Gone are the days when a new model took just six or nine months from design to "job one" rolling off the line. Gone too are the days when timber and canvas and flat sheet were the content of hand-built car bodies.

## Birth of a modern car

Preparation for a new model needed little else than a nod from the men at the top holding the purse strings. Today a more lengthy campaign is necessary. With so many manufacturers vying for buyers, a new design has to be a sure hit *before* it leaves the factory as "Job 1"!

---

**The Royal Mews**
**Buckingham Palace, London S.W.1.**

The Royal Mews at Buckingham Palace show motor cars and horsedrawn carriages that have belonged to the British Royal Family. There are three of the former displayed, of which the most interesting is the Daimler 'Royal Phaeton' made for King Edward VII when Prince of Wales in 1900.

**The Transport Museum**
**Witham Street, Belfast, Northern Ireland.**

This museum concentrates mainly upon railway exhibits, but there are also many models, about 20 horsedrawn carriages, 10 motor cycles, six fire trucks, and 20 motor

cars. Probably the most interesting of the latter are the vehicles of Irish origin, notably the 1908 Chambers.

**Motor Cycle and Car Museum**
**Standford Hall, near Rugby, Warwicks.**

It is not widely known outside the Midlands that Standford Hall contains not only its famous collection of motor cycles, but also pictures, documents, antique furniture, costumes, kitchen utensils — and cars. There are now several of these, including an 1897 Hurtu and a 1920 Carden cyclecar. The motor cycles are, however, the main attraction; indeed Standford Hall now has one of the most important collections in the world.

**Royal Scottish Museum**
**Chambers Street, Edinburgh 1, Midlothian.**

The Hall of Power in this museum contains a Scottish-built Albion dogcart of 1900; the second of the breed built. There are also various engines on show. In the cellar are several more cars; also a number of motor cycles.

**Pembrokeshire Motor Museum**
**Garrison Theatre, Pembroke Dock, Pembrokeshire.**

Most of the exhibits in the Pembrokeshire Motor Museum are changed frequently. In addition to an interesting range of early cars, there are also bicycles and motor-cycles form the 1880-1930 period.

A new model's characteristics are checked over and over again by test rigs and "on location". Here, a new model's suspension is analysed — as well as the driver's seat no doubt!

Right: How cold can it get?

Nowadays, the mammoth task of creating and manufacturing a new car can take three to four years from the initial concept to seeing the first version coming off a production line. There are many stages in the continuing cycle but each new model is born out of what is commonly called "market research".

## Crystal ball gazing

Detailed studies are made by special teams of future buyer requirements, of market spending habits which vary from country to country. Each potential export market also has its own legal and safety requirements which must be considered. Future economic conditions and personal income forecasts also play a large part in deciding whether, for example, a new model should be large, powerful and luxurious (suitable if a buoyant economic situation is forecast) or whether a small, low-priced, economical saloon should be added to the range. The mid-1970's, with statutory wage limitations, high mortgage interests, etc. — plus oil shortages — seem to have small cars favoured.

Styling trends and performance requirements are also subjected to analysis and study, and the number of variations — how many engine options should be introduced, how many interior trim choices should be offered, should estate and van models be incorporated into the range?

## Over to product development

The basic needs and variations investigated, another team looks into the future that the basic outline for the new model might have, and how the manufacturer can cope with the new production requirements.

This is work for the Product Development Department whose task it is to investigate the sales potential of the outline brief given to them for the new model, and what its exterior and interior measurements will have to be in order to include all that the brief lays down.

All this is fine, but the new model must also prove herself to be saleable at a competitive price — or have such advanced concepts incorporated that she can overcome being a little more expensive than similarly-sized vehicles from other makers.

Objectives are therefore set down for the new car's performance, her weight, size and pricing.

But all this may look fine on paper — can the manufacturer in fact cope with producing the car? The Product Development Group has to look into proposed manufacturing facilities, the cost of any new plant and machinery which will be needed, and also new factory areas required to cope with production.

Then there could be problems with staff to make the car — has the manufacturer enough labour to look after the new model or will more men be needed?

Finally, the Group has to cost out the building of prototype models, and give appraisals as to the amount of time and money involved in testing new items to be incorporated into the car (perhaps a new type of engine or a different type of suspension unit).

All this done, and the firm's management having a huge dossier of reports, costings, and statistics to study and approve, another department moves in on the scene.

## Let styling begin

Now is the time that the new model starts to receive something of an identity. Engineers prepare scale drawings and artists' impressions of the main mechanical items of the car (the engine unit, front and rear suspension systems, the wheel base of the vehicle, overall length that will be necessary to house these and also be able to include the previous briefs covering passenger room, boot size, headroom and so on. All this goes through to the styling department and body design starts to take shape.

What seems to be an endless barrage of possible design concepts hits the technical director's desk. It is his job to cut these down to a short list of possibles and probables and try to get the best out of each suggestion — eventually, after much discussion and many meetings with senior company executives, all angles from design feasibility to studying the possibilities of coping with new or unusual metal and plastics engineering seems to point to *a* design, *the* design.

Models will have been made to scale in order to help those responsible for the final styling choice to come to a decision.

## . . . To full scale models

Full-scale impressions are then built in clay on a wooden framework. The design studios are often elaborately equipped, for a mistake made at this stage, which might go unnoticed, could well be very expensive to put right later.

Even a new car's horn needs testing. Recordings of pitch, tone and decibels (noise levels) are taken.

Finalising detail of car body's design.

To give you some idea of what a design studio is like, let's take a look at one of the most up-to-date areas — Ford's Dunton, Essex, Design and Research Centre.

How many people are involved in the design work? You'd probably be astonished to learn that a team of some 2,000 work on new model styling! There are something like 45,000 square feet of space available for modelling and studios where three special tracks enable scale models to be built to exacting accuracy and within fine tolerances.

Each of these tracks has a length of 80 feet and is equipped with measuring "bridges" so that up to five models on each track can be measured accurately.

How accurately can these measuring bridges work to? Well, like those used by some other manufacturers, Ford's measure to within 1/10,000th of an inch, to keep a precise check on every shape of every surface.

In order to allow easier working at the final stages, the clay models can be transferred to special turntables where they can be seen from every possible angle in order to check that the design does not suffer when looked at from strange positions.

The first clay models produced in the design studios, are fitted with simulated windscreens and windows in perspex so that senior management can appraise the new model.

From these moulds checking fixtures are produced to check the contours of the actual glass.

Areas, such as floor and dash panels, which require special study by tool designers, are also produced in clay to allow early tool design and so reduce costly engineering changes at a later stage.

Royalite (plastic) models are produced for review by the Structures Design committee who check the model through successive development stages to assess space available for exhausts, fuel lines, brakes, fuel tanks, and suspensions.

The models are manufactured on vacuum-forming tools, which are softwood forms fabricated on metal panels and made to undimensioned layouts and sketches. They allow easy modification and are readily adaptable to meet changing requirements during development.

Royalite models are also used to provide panels, half-body assemblies, underbody and engine bays for the various departments to assess.

Interior trim is simulated on inner doors by use of grained plastic panels, and mock-ups are provided for the development of seating, steering pedal locations, mirrors, sun visors, and heaters, among other components. All are incorporated into a composite "buck" of the interior passenger departments used as a space development model.

The main equipment used in such a department as this includes an 8 feet by 6 feet by 5 feet electrical oven and a vacuum forming table to cover the largest Royalite plastic panel. They also have facilities for deep drawing, and plastic welding guns for the assembly of the panels.

After the Royalite models have been approved, construction and development of tooling aids follow to enable *metal* prototype bodies to be built. Production fixtures, dies and jigs allow accurate checking of panels when the model goes into production.

After the basic design has been agreed between prototype tool designers and other areas, model-makers construct templates and produce wooden hammer forms for the production of metal prototype panels by sheetmetal workers, and wooden jigs for panel checking.

## Plastic Moulds

The plastics section produces moulds from full size clay models and manufactures plastic reproductions of wheel trims, doorhandles, lamps, instrument panels, wheels, and radiator grilles for management appraisal.

The Die Keller Model Section manufactures plastic forms for use with Kellering machines which produce final production tooling for panels, and plastic jigs are made as checking fixtures by Quality Control.

The plastic styling moulds are also used to produce facing cores for hammer forms, used to finalise sheetmetal parts.

And so our prototype car arrives to a "viewing courtyard" — probably one of the most guarded and well-screened areas of any car design studio's area. Here, top management will be invited to view the new model, looking as good as if she had been made in the factory and complete with all her appendages fitted — trims, windscreen, bumpers, and so on.

The clay model and the prototype road vehicles which will be made to her design will probably be the most expensive cars ever built but will never be sold!

## Testing on the road and off

Once the prototypes have been accepted, it would seem fairly natural to consider starting production. But before this can get the go-ahead, the prototypes have a serious job of work to do. They cover thousands of miles in this country and many others to prove that the design

A seating buck developed for Ford's Escort.

is suitable for use in all types of climate and under normal and abnormal conditions.

## Testing to destruction

Back at home, rigs will be set up at the manufacturer's test area to simulate extremes of use. A door hinge may be rigged up to open and shut day in and day out for weeks on end to simulate use during, say, several years normal life span. Only when performance objectives are met do the parts get the final OK.

As parts are passed, they are costed and the Product Development Group is advised of the comparison against original targets set down.

Every manufacturer spends something like three years developing a new model. When you start to look at a car's construction, her mechanical parts, electrical system, suspension, and interior styling, it is not hard to see why it takes this long. And when you consider that every new part has to undergo extensive individual testing before being passed, then this time seems all too short.

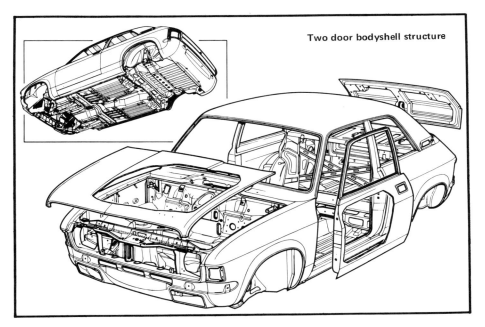

Two door bodyshell structure

*Allegro*

Super four door model

## A case for the marketing boys

Marketing staff, in collaboration with an advertising agency, work on ideas to give the new model enough impetus to be accepted by her new Public — the people who, it is hoped, will buy the latest model and make her a winner in her class. This involves all aspects of what is termed "the media": advertising in the local and national newspapers, in motoring magazines, on television, showroom placards, sales literature and brochures, and possibly feature films for Motor Shows throughout the world.

The Service Department will, at the same time, be producing dealers' maintenance manuals, to ensure that the new model will be correctly repaired and serviced.

## The first cars are built

Meanwhile, back at the factory, a "Functional Build" programme is initiated which allows a few "sample" cars to be run down the line and to allow outside suppliers to receive the final go-ahead to supply parts in large quantities ready for production. And as a final check, to see that nothing on the manufacturing side has been overlooked and that everything is feasible,

a "Pilot Build" scheme is introduced to the factory. If this shows no problems then the Product Development Group gives the model her "sign-off" papers and full-scale production is started.

If the manufacturer has factories in other countries which will be assisting with production of cars for their own and other local markets, parts are packed into crates so that they can be shipped out for assembly on arrival.

Spare parts are also distributed to dealers so that they have stocks ready and waiting on the shelves should new owners need them.

## What the papers say

The dealers will also be invited along to look at the new model. And writers and journalists will be encouraged to test the car so that they can pass on their findings as soon as the car is released and is on display in the dealers' showrooms.

After the dealers have received their display and demonstration fleets, the new model is announced to us, the general public and the manufacturer will await our response to the new car. Really, she's three year's old when you think about it!

And then the whole cycle starts again!

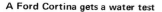

**A Ford Cortina gets a water test**

Ford cars coming off the production line at Trafford Park, Manchester.

# Getting to know . . .
# THE PRODUCTION LINE

"LITERALLY A SCIENCE of its own" is the way the production line has been described. It seems amazing that from the manufacturer's own resources, and those of his many outside suppliers come something like 2,000 individual items. All mate up in a pre-determined sequence to produce the vehicle which you or I buy without so much as a thought for what has gone into the making of her.

The list of materials incorporated into the many parts of the modern car makes interesting reading!

## Lets start at the foundry

Ford Motor Company has its own foundries which make many of the castings necessary for engines, transmissions and so on, though some parts are still likely to be brought in from outside sub-contractors.

A visit to a car manufacturer's foundry is exciting. To see the moulten metal being poured from the furnace's "cupola" (a huge ladle) into smaller ladles from which a sample is taken before the moulten metal is poured into the castings, is a sight which is difficult to forget.

From the foundry, castings are taken for machining and final preparation. If holes have to be drilled the casting will be fed into what is called a "transfer machine" where the casting will be automatically transferred through a series of machining and drilling stages. There can be as many as fifty individual drilling, reaming, tapping and machining operations set up automatically.

As all the engine and transmission parts come off the line, they are shipped into the engine or transmission build lines where mainly unskilled labour is used to bolt on the various parts, insert pistons and so forth into the engine castings. After spray painting and testing, engines, gearboxes and transmissions pass through to the Assembly plant to await the arrival of other parts from different manufacturing areas such as the body panel plant.

Metal Pouring at the Ford Motor Company Foundry, Dagenham.

The Press Shop at Ford's Halewood Body Plant. One of the largest in Britain with nearly 150 presses, the plant stamps and contours body panels for Ford's Escort and Capril Mk II models at pressures up to 2,000 tons. The inset shows rolls of steel which will be pressed into body panels.

## ... on to painting

Inspection for body repairs, finishing and wash-degreasing, is then carried out before immersion into a huge tank of priming paint. Most manufacturers now use the electrostatic painting process which charges the car with a positive charge and the paint with a negative electrical charge.

The paint in the bath rushes to stick to the positively charged metal of the car body giving it a perfect coating without overcoating.

The first priming coat is normally a red one followed by a grey one — though different manufacturers have different systems.

The car then has to pass through a large gas-fired baking oven where the paint is hardened off before top coats are sprayed on. Once again, this paint system — the one you see when you take delivery of a new car — has to be dried off in some way, probably by passing through a steam or gas-heated oven. Though special paint systems under investigation in America have been found to dry off within seconds of application, most manufacturers' cars use a more conventional top finish which needs approximately an hour to dry.

## Body panels from steel sheets

The manufacture of a car body can be done in several ways. The most commonly used form of construction is known as the unitary method of construction whereby huge pressed-steel parts make up the floor pans, the roof and bonnet panels, boot lids, and four wing sections.

Each sheet metal part starts life as a flat piece of steel to the required gauge and specification. From this point on, it doesn't stand a chance! From the car's drawings are made up special tooling equipment which will form the metal into various shapes as it passes through a line of gigantic presses. The presses are often the equivalent of two storeys in height and need very sound foundations. The presses will often go down the equivalent of one floor where all the metal scrap trimmings will be delivered to be taken away for scrap.

With pressures exerted on the metal of up to 2,000lb wouldn't you bend a little! After one operation, the first

16

LEFT: Two men work together in a part of the vast Ford Halewood Body Plant. Their jobs involve the sub-assembly of body parts.

BELOW: A Ford Escort is jigged into position, operators press their buttons for action and this huge multiwelder comes to life spot-welding the various parts together.

pressing is put through the next stage which may put in another shape, or perhaps have its edges bent over and guillotined off. The next press in the line may punch out holes for windows in a door panel, or holes for lamps in the front and rear sections and so forth.

Following inspection the parts then pass on for sub-assembly. Here each part is set up in a jig. Once the basic superstructure and under-body sections are in place they are spot-welded to hold their positions before passing on to a large machine which completes the welding job of the entire structure in one quick and painless operation. Whether the underbody and super-structure of the car are welded up separately or as one unit depends on the design and on the manufacturer. Once the wings are welded into position the production

The body of the car goes through a line where any small imperfections in the metalwork are put right before paint dipping.

line starts to work in earnest and monorail systems overhead start feeding the assembly workers with doors, boots, bonnets . . .

## On the trim line

Still looking rather sorry for herself, our car, wheel-less and engine-less, continues along the production line. As with the colour choice, a computer which has had the customer's order fed into it, decides which trim — standard, deluxe or whatever may be available — should be fitted. Slowly items are fed along and amass alongside the line as the car continues her journey — the necessary electrical components, the interior headlining, the front grille and light assemblies, windows and winder mechanisms, door trims, and windscreen.

Several steps along and other production line workers will be waiting with the steering column, the horns and all the under-the-bonnet regalia necessary. Then the

door handles, and electrical wiring looms ready connected perhaps to the instrument panel and fascia. Over 200 feet of electrical cable, all colour-coded to a standard pattern to make wiring up of the car more easy, starts to get passed through the engine compartment bulkhead so that it is ready and waiting for the engine, gearbox and transmission which has been progressing in a jig elsewhere and timed to be fed into the trimline at the right moment, right under the correct body (provided the computer is doing its job correctly).

As it comes along and the body is lowered down, men will start to bolt up the suspension units on the lower part to the body which has come to meet it. Brake pipes are linked up, electrics "plugged" in and items like windscreen wipers fitted. Steering wheel, clutch, brake

and accelerator pedals and any other interior trim necessary, including carpeting, nearly completes our car.

## Let her roll . . .

But we are still wheel-less! Along from the wheel-making and tyre fitting areas come ready-to-bolt-on wheel units complete with the correct size and type of tyre.

Well, at least she's able to roll on her own wheels now (and there's a spare tyre in the boot). But we don't seem to have any seats . . . come on computer, that's it. Right type, right colour . . . and they're fitted.

A few last checks remain to be carried out — to the suspension and steering settings. All the necessary fluids have been put into the correct reservoirs, and grease has been applied where required. Water in the radiator and just a gallon of petrol necessary then . . . ignition (provided no-one has forgotten to put the battery in!).

A final safety check is carried out and she goes on to the special "rolling road" which can be used to simulate various speeds to check that all is well at various engine revs, that the accelerator, brakes, lights, steering, wipers, horn, indicators, and so on are in working order.

After a brief road test, sometimes not now made as the rolling road often suffices in pointing to potential troubles, and our car is given the embarrassment of a cold shower — jets of water pour gallons upon gallons of water from all directions over her bodywork. In all she suffers the indignity of bombardment from about 400 gallons in about four minutes of water at pressures up to 50 pounds per square inch (dependant upon the manufacturer).

A check is made for leaks and if all is waterproof, off

information, normally presented in a convenient and readable form, is very useful should you be given an examination project to do!

LEFT:
After the primer, undercoats are sprayed on before baking in an oven. Top coats follow but these are applied by hand. Then the engine and suspension feed into the line complete with front suspension. Then final trimming-out and our Escort gets her wheels.

goes the car for a dry-off and to join the queue awaiting transporter lorries to come and give them their first taste of the open road — albeit by piggy-back to the dealer whose customer will be awaiting her arrival with some anticipation. He probably will not realise how many people have been involved in her creation, that approximately 80 hours is spent making her parts, and just 22 hours or so in her construction on the line.

The Sunday Times' artist's impression of "How a Car is Made" depicts the production line sequence better than words can.

It may be worth considering a visit to a car manufacturer's plant one day. Most of the larger manufacturers are more than willing to welcome school and college parties, youth clubs, car clubs and so on.

Most manufacturers also have invaluable information available (needless to say, covering their own products) for those who want to get to know more. This

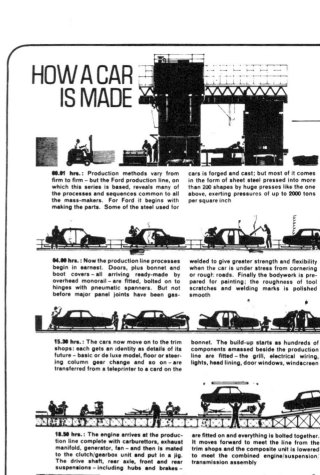

## HOW A CAR IS MADE

**00.01 hrs.:** Production methods vary from firm to firm – but the Ford production line, on which this series is based, reveals many of the processes and sequences common to all the mass-makers. For Ford it begins with making the parts. Some of the steel used for cars is forged and cast; but most of it comes in the form of sheet steel pressed into more than 200 shapes by huge presses like the one above, exerting pressures of up to 2000 tons per square inch

**04.00 hrs.:** Now the production line processes begin in earnest. Doors, plus bonnet and boot covers – all arriving ready-made by overhead monorail – are fitted, bolted on to hinges with pneumatic spanners. But not before major panel joints have been gas- welded to give greater strength and flexibility when the car is under stress from cornering or rough roads. Finally the bodywork is pre- pared for painting; the roughness of tool scratches and welding marks is polished smooth

**15.30 hrs.:** The cars now move on to the trim shops: each gets an identity as details of its future – basic or de luxe model, floor or steer- ing column gear change and so on – are transferred from a teleprinter to a card on the bonnet. The build-up starts as hundreds of components amassed beside the production line are fitted – the grill, electrical wiring, lights, head lining, door windows, windscreen

**18.50 hrs.:** The engine arrives at the produc- tion line complete with carburettors, exhaust manifold, generator, fan – and then is mated to the clutch/gearbox unit and put in a jig. The drive shaft, rear axle, front and rear suspensions – including hubs and brakes – are fitted on and everything is bolted together. It moves forward to meet the line from the trim shops and the composite unit is lowered to meet the combined engine/suspension/ transmission assembly

**20.20 hrs.:** Five matching wheels slot down and are bolted on, and the car rolls forward on its own feet for the first time. Fuel is added to the tank and the car at last springs to life. Seats are the last item to be added to the interior. The engine idles as it is checked; then the car is driven to the tracking station, where suspension and steering settings are adjusted and checked. After a final examination of the trim the car is passed (or rejected) before it goes on to the roller testing station

# WHAT GOES IN...

| | |
|---|---|
| **Aluminium** | Engine parts, transmission parts, spark plugs, castings, trim mouldings |
| **Asbestos** | Brake linings, gaskets, sound deadeners |
| **Barite** | Fillers for paints, rubber, plastics |
| **Bauxite** | Ore for metal aluminium |
| **Beeswax** | Wire insulation, adhesives |
| **Bismuth** | Hardens lead, tin, steel |
| **Borax** | For smelting and special steels |
| **Cadmium** | Alloy to harden copper, electropainting, paints |
| **Carbon** | Rubber making, paints, electrodes, graphite seals, electrical brushes |

| | |
|---|---|
| **Cattle** | Glue, glycerines, hides, hair for air cleaners |
| **Chemicals** | Nylon, synthetic rubber, plastics |
| **Chromite** | Ore produces chromium used for plating, alloys |
| **Clay** | Rubber filler, modelling |
| **Coal** | Iron and steel making, nylon, solvents, tars, fuel |
| **Cobalt** | Steel making |
| **Coconut Oil** | Paints, lacquers |
| **Columbium** | Stainless steel |
| **Copper** | Electrical system, radiator, plated parts, alloys |
| **Cork** | Gaskets, insulation |
| **Cotton** | Wadding, padding, felt, tyres, insulation, thread |

| | |
|---|---|
| **Diamonds** | Cutting, grinding, drilling metals |
| **Flaxseed** | Linseed oil for paint, sand binder in foundry |
| **Fluorspar** | Flux in iron and steel making |
| **Glass** | Windscreen, windows, head- lights and spun insulation |
| **Gold** | Ornament plating |
| **Hides** | Upholstery, belts |
| **Iron Ore** | Steel, castings for engine and chassis parts |
| **Jute** | Fabric, floor coverings |
| **Lead** | Batteries, petrol, solder, plating |
| **Lime** | Flux in steelmaking, lubricant in wire making |

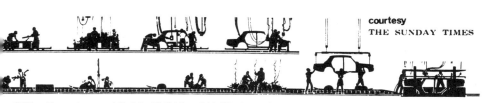

courtesy
THE SUNDAY TIMES

**03.00 hrs.:** The pressings are carried by fork lift trucks to the pre-production line workshops – and in separate processes the building of the superstructure and underbody begins. First, small sub-assemblies are put together by spot welding. Then these are fitted into jigs, which hold the pieces in place as they are fed into automatic welders; from these the major superstructure and underbody units emerge complete. At the upper level in our diagram, the men are tack-welding together the roof, sides and scuttle of the car; at the lower level the underbody is taking shape. Finally the superstructure and underbody come together, the wings are fitted and the whole unit is welded together. At one stage the car is inverted in a roll-over jig for stitch-welding to take place

**09.00 hrs.:** Before the paint is put on the car gets a complete washing, inside and out; all joints are covered with a sealer and gas welds painted over. Then the underbody is dipped waist-high in an epoxy resin bath which gives an anti-corrosive finish to metal and seals the drainage channels. Priming coats are sprayed on by hand – a red primer first, and, before it is dry, a grey primer. The cars pass through a gas-fired oven for 40 minutes, then each body is wet-sanded with demineralised water and dried. Now three top colour coats are sprayed on; beside the line a teleprinter taps out the colour or colour combination for each car based on an analysis of orders from dealers and overseas distributors which has already been completed. Drying takes an hour as the cars move slowly through a steam-heated oven

**16.40 hrs.:** Into the car, too, go the horns, battery, brake fluid reservoirs, steering column, radiator and pipes – all under-the-bonnet parts. The instrument panel is fitted, and from it sprout the lengths of bright coloured wiring and tubes which will soon be connected to the engine. Finally a few more externals are put on – chrome fittings, door handles and catches

**19.20 hrs.:** The nearly completed car now moves along a raised line. Above are fitted the rear-view mirror, wipers and interior trim; the radiator is filled and hydraulic fluid fed into the brake and clutch systems. Underneath everything is connected up – oil, petrol and brake pipes, steering, pedals – and a gear lever is added. The laying of carpets and mats almost completes the trim

**22.00 hrs.:** The car is driven on the rollers – testing the engine, transmission, steering, brakes and lights. If declared safe, it goes for a brief road test. After this comes the water test; the car is sprayed with 36 streams of water at 50 lb. per square inch pressure – a total of 400 gallons bombarded in four minutes – to check for leaks. Dried down, it has its final check; then it's parked in the trade lines to await the delivery driver and the trip to market

Rolling road . . .
and leak test

Final inspection

| | | | |
|---|---|---|---|
| Magnesite | Mineral ore of magnesium | Plastics | Body and engine parts, trim, upholstery |
| Magnesium | Light alloys for engine parts | | |
| Manganese | Steel making | Platinum | Alloy for special wire, electric contact points, transistors |
| Mercury | Mirrors, amalgams with other metals, switches | | |
| | | Rubber | May be natural or synthetic. Tyres, weatherproofing, vibration damping, belts, insulations, hoses, windscreen wipers |
| Mica | Electrical insulators | | |
| Mohair | Upholstery, carpets | | |
| Molybdenum | Steel alloys, fine wire, grease, paint | | |
| Nickel | Alloy with steel, copper, other metals, plating | Silver | Electrical system, plating, brazing |
| Paint | Body and interior finish | Sisal | Seat padding |
| Paper | Insulation, gaskets, sound-proofing, filters | Steel | Frame body, wheels, engine parts, gears, springs, hardware |
| Petroleum | Petrol, oil, lubricants, synthetics, solvents | Sugar Cane | Alcohol, Cellulose for safety glass, solvent in varnishes |

| | |
|---|---|
| Sulphur | Vulcanising rubber, lubricant, additives, steel |
| Textiles | Upholstery, lining, tyres |
| Tin | Plating, alloys, solder |
| Tungsten | Special steel, lamp filaments |
| Turpentine | Paints |
| Vanadium | Special steel |
| Wheat Straw | Strawboards, panels |
| Wood | Cellulose for safety glass, packing cases, paper, fibre board, truck body parts |
| Wool | Upholstery, carpeting, felt |
| Zinc | Batteries, alloy for die-cast parts, plating |
| Zirconium | Alloy in steel and copper making, aluminium castings |

21

THE CAR has become such an everyday sight that most of its several thousand parts are merely accepted as "being there" — somewhere. Not least in this respect is that most vital piece of engineering the "engine". This word alone, defined in the dictionary as 'a mechanical contrivance consisting of several parts', could not be *less* complimentary!

# Getting to know . . .
# ENGINES

Look into the engine compartment of a car and it will take on an awesome look, an appearance of being a highly intricate and complicated piece of mechanical engineering. And when you consider that what the eye can see is only the tip of the iceberg, so to speak, the car engine does indeed give the impression of something very technical needing a highly trained person to understand its workings.

But a logical approach to understanding the different types of engine being produced for the modern production car of today will soon allow us to appreciate the job it does, and how it does it.

From the earliest dawn of practical power for cars, the piston engine has had an almost unrivalled existence and received a high quota of development. Needless to say the piston engine variants in use today will be around for some time to come, though in even more developed stages of refinement to combat pollution and other environmental hazards.

There are sure to be, however, strong competition from "newcomers" to the under-bonnet power game. During the past year or so we have seen much publicity given to the lack of world fuel and this has given slow but necessary impetus to designers, engineers and the more inventive motor magnates to come up with possible solutions.

As early as 1950 the Rover Company had developed a gas turbine car engine. It was built into a road car and went through many and various trials at the hands of professional drivers, celebrities and influential people. Prince Philip was one to take the wheel of a Rover gas turbine car, the first of which had the distinguishing registration number of JET 1. The Science Museum in London have the car on display.

Rover was not the only company to investigate the possibilities of the gas turbine — the futuristic Etoile Filante, a single-seater used as a test bed by the Renault Company in 1956, was another. The American Chrysler Company has experimented in the gas turbine field.

But for reasons of weight, practicability and economy, gas turbine engines are not likely to rival the piston engine on our roads.

## Electric Power?

What about the cleanest form of "fuel" around though? Could electrically-powered cars be the piston engine's challenger?

As long ago as 1966, Ford's research staff were given a brief to look into the possibilities of producing a small electric car for use in cities and busy towns.

There has been much interest in such a development ever since, and one small firm has been building a "production" electric vehicle since the early seventies. Enfield Automotive Limited won a contract to build 61 experimental cars. Financial backing for this project came from The Electricity Council who intended to provide the cars to some of their meter readers to use on their rounds! Called the Enfield 8000, this two-seater, smaller than a Mini but costing about £3,000, seems to have a limited but nonetheless important future.

Perhaps, one day, we shall pull into a garage of the future and ask for a recharge for the car's batteries, but until then, the internal combustion engine will probably remain supreme.

## Internal Combustion Engines Today

The majority of cars today have a four-stroke petrol engine and though there are several different forms depending on the number of cylinders, how these cylinders are laid out, and their operation (by the older push-rod system or by the more direct method of camshafts), their principle of operation remains the same.

So let's have a look at the main components of a modern internal combustion engine each part of which performs a vital interconnecting link in providing the engine as a whole with its power.

The largest and hence heaviest item is the cylinder block which is usually allied to the crankcase. Being normally a large and heavy component made from cast iron, high performance engines (such as those found in sports and racing car engines) often use a lighter material. In such engines an aluminium alloy casting is used, the cylinders themselves being inserts of cast iron set into the aluminium alloy cylinder block.

An equally beefy casting (in cast iron or aluminium alloys) is the cylinder head which has to be separable from the cylinder block. To make the joining surface between each thoroughly gas tight a gasket is used.

This gasket seal may appear somewhat flimsy and soft being made from thin copper sheet and asbestos or similar materials, but it is essential for the efficiency of cylinders. If an engine is air-cooled, then the gasket merely seals the gas pressure created. If the engine is water-cooled, the gasket also provides a watertight seal.

Most engines today are in fact water-cooled. There are air-cooled engines about like those used in the Volkswagen Beetle, but the water-cooled engine is far more widely used.

In such an engine both cylinder block and the cylinder head have waterway passages through them. Water can pass through these pasages in order to cool parts which otherwise reach unacceptably high temperatures.

One drawback of the water-cooled engine is that in cold climates, the water, acting as an engine coolant, can freeze. During winter months an anti-freeze solution has to be added to the water in the correct proportions to prevent freeze-ups and the nasty consequences following a rapid thaw.

Air-cooled units such as those in the Volkswagen "Beetle" and several European-built small cars, have cool air blown over the cylinder block and head which are normally made with many small fins to assist in dissipating the unwanted heat.

## The Cylinder Head

What is the function of the cylinder head?

First, it provides what we shall see later is the necessary combustion space for the cylinders. On some of the latest engines in production, combustion takes place not in the cylinder head, but in a depression in the top of the piston itself.

Next, the cylinder head provides a means of locating the valves (inlet and outlet) for each cylinder — that is, in the overhead valve engine. Side-valve engines were popular at one time (for example, they were fitted to the 'sit-up-and-beg' Ford Popular).

Valves control the flow of gases both in and out of the cylinders and with their associated gear are probably the most sensitive parts of the engine. Any valve inefficiency will seriously decrease the power coming from the engine.

The inlet and exhaust valves are operated by the camshaft which normally finds its place in the cylinder block or above the cylinder head.

The camshaft then, operates the inlet and exhaust valves. In overhead valve engines, except those with overhead camshafts, the lift from the cams is transmitted to the valves via pushrods that run up the side of the cylinder block and rockers and tappets in the cylinder head.

In overhead camshaft engines there are usually two camshafts fitted. These are situated above the inlet valves to one side and the outlet valves on the other and transmit their power to the valves *via* small cylindrical slides. Being more direct this system allows higher revving for performance engines.

Why is the cylinder block (including the cylinder head and the crankcase) necessarily such a heavy component — the major part of the engine's construction in fact?

The cylinder block, as we have seen, forms a rather complex piece of engineering which has to stand up to all the major strains which will be imposed, incorporating as it does the cylinders in which the pistons fly up and down. And whether the engine is a four, six or even 12-cylinder type, pistons travel up and down the cylinder walls at a phenomenal rate — for every mile a car travels, each piston will travel twice that in its journey up and down the cylinder's bore.

The crankshaft positioned in the crank case and normally forming part of the cylinder block assembly has the job of revolving at anything up to 6,000 revolutions per minute (R.P.M.), converting the up-and-down movement of the pistons into circular movement. In high performance engines this could be as much as 8,000 r.p.m.

Being the mainstay of the engine, the cylinder block and crankcase are the components to which are fitted the engine's ancillary items and other engine components.

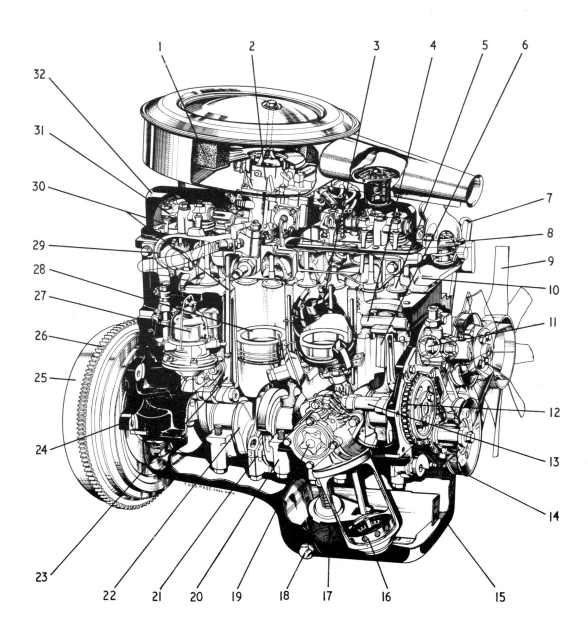

KEY

1. Air Filter
2. Carburettor
3. Distributor
4. Gudgeon Pin (Little End)
5. Valve
6. Con Rod (Takes Piston Power to Crankshaft)
7. Oil Dipstick
8. Thermostat
9. Fan
10. Water Gallery (in cylinder head)
11. Water Pump
12. Timing Chain (Drive from Crankshaft to Camshaft)
13. Camshaft
14. Fan Belt (Drives Fan, Water Pump & Generator)
15. Oil Sump
16. Oil Filter
17. Oil Strainer & Pick-Up
18. Oil Drain Plug
19. Oil Pump
20. Main Bearing Cap
21. Big End
22. Crankshaft
23. Cam Follower
24. Cylinder Block
25. Flywheel
26. Starter Ring
27. Fuel Pump with Filter
28. Piston
29. Exhaust Manifold
30. Push Rods
31. Valve Rocker
32. Rocker Cover

## What part do pistons play?

Basically, the pistons travel up and down inside the cylinder bores and, dependent on which "Cycle" is underway, suck in, compress or exhaust the fuel mixture. As we shall see later when we look at the four-stroke cycle in more detail, the piston bears the full brunt of the force which is generated by the combustion of the gas under pressure.

The pistons travel up and down in the cylinder bores in the cylinder block, and are linked to the crankshaft by connecting rods.

The connecting rods are attached at their upper ends (or "small ends") to the undersides of the pistons. The lower ends (which are colloquially termed the "big ends") connect to the crankshaft, which, as we have said, converts the pistons' up and down movements into circular motion.

The crankshaft is so geared that it in turn actuates the camshaft which turns at half the speed of the crankshaft and in turn operates the valves.

## The Four-Stroke Cycle

That all sounds very involved, but the drawings will help to show us the way all these parts inter-relate to give drive to the car (page 24).

The first stage of the four-stroke cycle shows the piston beginning to travel down the cylinder bore. This action of the piston causes the camshaft to open the *inlet* valve.

As the inlet valve opens, the downward movement of our piston creates "suck", so pulling in a petrol-and-air mixture from the "carburettor". So, the first turn of the crankcase has drawn the piston down the cylinder and we have a mixture of petrol and air in the cylinder chamber.

When the piston reaches the bottom of the cylinder the camshaft closes the inlet valve to our particular cylinder.

We now have a petrol and air mixture trapped in the cylinder bore.

But the cycle must continue — so the piston starts its return back up the bore, compressing the trapped mixture as it goes.

The cylinder now contains a trapped, compressed mixture which, because of its highly explosive ratio of petrol and air, can be ignited inside the cylinder by the high voltage spark from the sparking plug.

The mixture, once ignited, burns quickly creating a tremendous pressure. Now something must give way to this sudden pressure — the piston. So the piston is forced back down the bore of the cylinder and stage three of the cycle, the power stroke, is completed.

Somehow, the burnt gas must be released from the cylinder bore and this is done as the piston reaches the bottom of its stroke and the camshaft opens the *exhaust* valve. The burnt gases are forced out through the exhaust valve as the piston travels once more up the bore. And the piston returns to start another cycle.

The complete cycle can be summarised as:

> **Stage 1: Induction:** (when the petrol/air mixture is "sucked into the cylinder).
>
> **Stage 2: Compression:** (when the inflow of petrol and air is shut off and the piston comes up the cylinder to compress the mixture).
>
> **Stage 3: Power Stroke:** (when the volatile mixture is ignited by a high powered spark).
>
> **Stage 4: Exhaust:** (when the exhaust valve opens, reducing pressure in the cylinder and the rising piston pushes out the spent gases).

Taking a four-cylinder engine — such as the Ford Escort or the BLMC 1300 — the order that the cylinders are fired is so arranged that each is providing one of the stages we have just seen in the four-stroke cycle. For example, one cylinder will have its piston sucking in the fuel/air mixture from the carburettor. The next cylinder's piston will have already completed this stage and will be compressing the mixture. The third cylinder will be at the stage when the spark from the sparking plug combusts the mixture, while the fourth cylinder will be on the exhaust stroke emitting the spent gases after firing.

No matter how many cylinders an engine has, the principle is always the same. The point on the credit side for multi-cylinder engines is that more power can be produced from a less-bulky, smoother-running power plant.

## Other Important parts of the Engine

We have seen how the basic parts of the engine function in relation to each other. But there are several other items of equipment needed to build up our engine into an operational power plant.

How is the petrol and air mixture carried from the carburettor? The p/a mixture from the carb is drawn into the cylinder (via the inlet manifold), through the inlet ports and valve openings. Since there is a need for both the inlet and exhaust of the gases, there is an inlet and an exhaust *manifold* to cope with each function.

The inlet manifold conveys the petrol and air mixture from the carburettor to the inlet ports. The exhaust manifold does a similar job by taking the spent gases away from the exhaust ports to the exhaust pipe which then runs underneath the car, and through a silencer, or group of silencers.

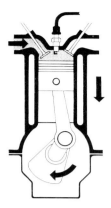

**1 Induction**: *The first half turn of the crankshaft draws the piston down the cylinder. At the same time the inlet valve opens and the petrol/air mixture is sucked into the cylinder.*

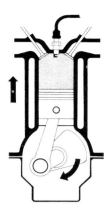

**2 Compression**: *On the next half turn of the crankshaft the inlet valve shuts and the piston slides up the cylinder, compressing the mixture.*

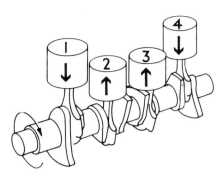

*This diagram, showing the crankshaft with pistons and connecting rods, indicates how the firing order is obtained. No. 1 piston is just starting the induction stroke and will continue through the cycle with compression, power and exhaust strokes. No. 3 has just finished induction and has started compression. No. 4 has completed compression and is on the power stroke. No. 2 has just finished the first three strokes and is rising on the exhaust stroke.*

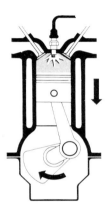

**3 Power**: *The spark at the plug ignites the mixture which burns rapidly, producing a large pressure rise. This forces the piston down the cylinder. The downward movement allows the gas to expand and pressure to fall.*

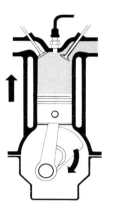

**4 Exhaust**: *The opening of the exhaust valve allows the pressure to fall to nearly atmospheric and the rising piston then forces out the burnt gas. When the piston reaches the top of its travel the exhaust valve shuts, the inlet valve opens and another cycle begins.*

The *carburettor's* job is to supply the correct mixture of petrol and air so that the engine can burn it efficiently. Although the principle of the carburettor is relatively simple, modern versions have become highly developed and complicated pieces of engineering.

Fuel stored in the car's petrol tank has to be fed through a delivery pipe to the carburettor. This is normally done by a pump which can be either electrically operated or of a mechanical type. The latter is normally operated by the engine's camshaft and so will be found located near it in the engine compartment. An electrical pump can be sited away from the engine area as it is independent of other mechanical parts. It can be positioned in the boot of the car, near the petrol tank for example.

# Getting to know . . .

# THE CARBURETTOR

THE ENGINE CAN only operate efficiently if the correct fuel to air ratio is being fed to the combustion chambers by the carburettor.

Early carburettors, such as the Siegfried Marcus type, were primitive but did work. Marcus' principle used a brush which revolved in the carburettor's small reservoir of petrol. The brush was driven round and round but being only partly submerged, flung off a fine spray of petrol in the form of a mist. This was then introduced to air in the mixing chamber from whence it was fed to an inlet valve and the engine cylinder.

Modern carburettors work on different principles today with the proportions of fuel to air being regulated by *jets* which control the amount of air in relation to a measured proportion of fuel. Normally the ratio is something in the order of 8,000 parts of air to one of petrol (by volume) — or 13 parts of air to one of petrol by weight. The correct ratio for each individual car is of critical importance not only to the engine's efficient operation, but of course to fuel consumption.

The system by which the correct amount of air is allowed to mix with the fuel is called the venturi principle. If a tube is used through which the air is passed, the air will travel from an area of high pressure to an area of low pressure. If our tube's bore is reduced in size at any point, then this acts as the venturi, and the pressure reduces, encouraging the flow of the air along the tube. The velocity of the gas increases due to the venturi causing this reduction in pressure.

Petrol from the petrol tank in the boot is pumped first through a fine filter to hold back any damaging sediments, and then to the carburettor's own "fuel tank" — a small reservoir bowl. The bowl contains a float which, as the level of fuel rises or falls controls a needle valve which in turn controls the inflow of topping-up fuel.

Now the venturi tube is sited alongside the reservoir of fuel (or float chamber) whose feed tube passes into the venturi.

As air flowing from the carburettor intake passes through the narrowing venturi section, the decrease in bore size reduces the pressure. This decrease in pressure caused by the venturi sucks in fuel from the float chamber feed tube — and into the air stream.

The float, meanwhile ensures that the feed tube to the venturi is always topped up.

How is the air flow regulated? The rate of the air flow can be increased by the driver by operating the car's accelerator pedal. So the more the small throttle butterfly valve is opened in the venturi, the greater the flow of air the more fuel is sucked in to make up the correct mixture.

The mixture then passes into the engine *via* the inlet manifolds and then to the valve ports in the cylinder head.

## A Delicate Instrument

As you can imagine, the carburettor is a precision-built piece of the car's equipment — rather like the heart and lungs of the car built into one. As such a finely set piece of engineering, it has to be protected from the invasion of even quite small particles of dust and dirt.

There could be filth in the petrol tank — so a fuel filter is set in the fuel line to hold any particles which might be damaging from reaching the float chamber.

Similarly, there could be all manner of foreign matter waiting to jump down the air inlet to the carburettor's venturi — so an air filter in the form, normally, of a large cylindrical or smaller "pancake" style filter is used to prevent harmful grit and dirt being passed into the engine.

We have seen how all the engine's parts inter-relate. Imagine, then, a harmful amount of grit coming in through the air stream mixing with the fuel, passing into the manifold, being sucked into the combustion chamber as the inlet valve opens and so on. It will find its

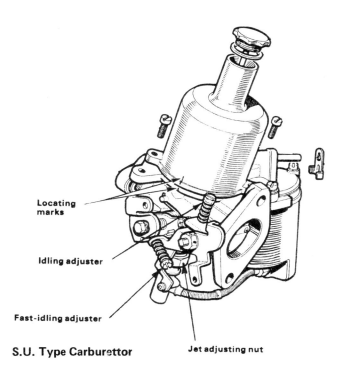

Locating marks

Idling adjuster

Fast-idling adjuster

**S.U. Type Carburettor**

Jet adjusting nut

way into the engine oil used to lubricate all the moving parts and damage their precision faced surfaces and cause severe engine wear.

There are several types of air filter and each does the same vital job — all too often unappreciated by the car owner. Whether the air filter is fitted with a replaceable paper element which slowly clogs up with unwanted dirt particles, or whether it has a wire gauze element soaked in oil to which the dust particles cling, they provide a simple yet effective barrier. But if ignored and allowed to get thoroughly dirty, then the fuel to air mixture will be altered and dirt will eventually find its harmful way around the engine.

## Twin Carburettors, Compound Carburettors . . .

Other than the fixed, and the variable jet types of carburettor, there are others such as the Weber Twin Choke (or Twin Barrel) model. The twin-choke carb has two large circular barrels sticking up. These are the air passages. Between the two barrels is a float chamber for the reservoir of fuel which is fed to each barrel at the same rate. Carburettors such as this are most commonly found on high performance sports cars. The initials TC will often give away a car fitted with twin carbs.

Yet another type of carburettor is the Compound Carburettor which incorporates two or more fixed choke barrels feeding a single manifold. This type of carburettor, made by such firms as Solex and Weber, is common equipment on American vehicles though some European high performance saloon cars also use them.

## And Look — No Carburettors . . .

After all we have seen, you'd assume that all equipment fitted as the makers badge and model mark the modern, high-powered racing car. Indeed the system of "petrol injection", which eliminates the need for carburettors to atomise the fuel, is also becoming popular on larger performance styled saloon cars.

You can often tell a car with petrol injection equipment fitted as the makers badge and model mark will usually **be** supplemented by the initials PI. The Triumph 2.5 PI is an example of a sporty saloon with petrol injection fitted. Fuel is fed in precisely metered doses to each of the car's six cylinders for smooth running and good acceleration.

With the injection system, petrol is literally squirted through a fine nozzle — one nozzle to each cylinder. With the help of a pump, the fuel is "injected" into the cylinders at great pressure.

Since no manifold is needed to carry fuel from a carburettor to the cylinders, you might think that fuel injection is the method to use. True, it gives improved performance, possible fuel savings since fuel is distributed more efficiently, and better response of the engine to the driver's throttle pressure. But the system is expensive, not only to install but to service should the need arise. There are both mechanical and electronic systems available, the latter being the ultimate in technical sophistication.

## Running Sweetly . . .

The efficient operation of a piston engine relies on all its many parts being in good condition, and correctly functioning. In addition, each part must be "timed" to

## TWO STROKE CYCLE

As used for engines in some Swedish Saab saloons, the Wartburg Knight, most motor cycles and scooters.

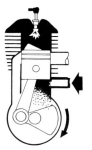

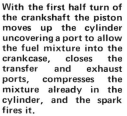

With the first half turn of the crankshaft the piston moves up the cylinder uncovering a port to allow the fuel mixture into the crankcase, closes the transfer and exhaust ports, compresses the mixture already in the cylinder, and the spark fires it.

The burning fuel mixture forces the piston down the cylinder to uncover the exhaust port, and the exhaust gases escape. At the same time the mixture in the crankcase is compressed and forced through the now open transfer port into the cylinder.

function at the correct moment and in the correct sequence. The carburettor's air-to-fuel ratio must be correct otherwise the fuel mixture will become too rich or conversely too lean and the performance will suffer, to say nothing of the fuel bill!

The valves, too, must be correctly adjusted so that their opening corresponds as closely as possible to the best practical time for each operation. In fact the theoretical optimum would be for the valves to open and close at the points when a piston is at the top of its stroke, or the bottom of the stroke. But theory is one thing, practice another.

Valve timing is the term used to refer to the position of the crankshaft's rotation at the particular moments when the valves are performing their vital opening and closing functions.

In practice the valves are timed to open fractionally earlier, and close fractionally later than the "top" or "bottom dead centre" positions of the pistons which we have said would seem to be theoretically the best. Taking a point marked on the crankcase, the valves are "timed" so many degrees before top dead centre (to open the valves) or so many degrees after bottom dead centre (to close) and so ensure that a greater amount of power can be obtained from the engine.

You may have heard also of "ignition timing". Like our theoretical best times for valve opening, it would be a good bet to assume that the best time for the sparking plug to emit its high voltage spark would be at the top dead centre piston position after the piston has just completed its compression stroke, and the mixture is ready for blast off.

But once again it is normal to adjust the ignition timing to ensure that the spark to the plugs to each cylinder is emitted just before the piston reaches its top dead centre position on the compression stroke. The ignition, like the valves, is timed to occur so many degrees of the crankshaft's rotation before this "tdc" point.

So we hear garage mechanics explaining to a confused motorists, wondering why his car has not been running sweetly, that the ignition needed "advancing" (altering to an earlier time) or "retarding" (adjusting to a later time) in relation to degrees of the crankshaft's rotation.

## What can the "Compression Ratio" tell us?

We have seen how the piston, on its second stage of the four-stroke cycle, compresses the volatile mixture of fuel and air which has been sucked in through the inlet valve by the piston's first movement down the cylinder bore. So "compression ratio" must have something to do with this second stage of the cycle.

A Ford BDA Engine showing fuel injectors in place of carburettor.

Compression ratio is the term which applies to the ratio of the volume above a piston to the volume above it at its lowest point — bottom dead centre. And the higher the compression ratio stated for an engine, the more power is exerted on the piston down on its power stroke. In this way, the compression ratio tells us how efficiently the heat and energy inherent in the fuel-air mixture is being used in the engine.

Most family saloons will be found to have a compression ratio of about 8, possibly 9 to 1.

Manufacturers' brochures normally give a pretty complete breakdown of their cars' performance figures. And it is in the technical specification that the compression ratio will be given. For example, Triumph Motors, part of the British Leyland group, list the following values for compression ratios:

Triumph Toledo — 8.5:1
Spitfire       — 9.0:1
TR6   P.I.    — 9.5:1

Triumph Spitfire Mk IV

# KEEPING COOL

ALL THE HEAT and power developed by a car's engine must somehow be kept to a comfortable and satisfactory level if parts are not to become overheated and become distorted and damaged. Lubrication oil passing around inside the engine, lubricating the many moving parts takes away some of the heat produced by say, the pistons and main bearings. But more of oil and lubrication later.

## Air Cooling

What other method of cooling can be used to dissipate all the unwanted heat? First, the engine can be cooled by air — rather like on air-cooled motor cycle engines. This is done normally by building hundreds of small fins into the castings which make up the main engine bulk and the airflow over them (and from a cooling fan for times when the car is moving slowly or idling) cools the engine down.

Air-cooled engines are popular on many foreign cars, despite their disadvantage of noisier operation. The Volkswagen "Beetle" has a well-proven air-cooled engine. The Volkswagen's engine is mounted at the rear of the car and uses a radial fan and special ducting to induce a strong, cooling airflow to the areas where the engine heat is generated — mainly the cylinders and heads. A thermostat is used to bring in the fan as soon as the engine's fins cannot cope with the dissipation of the heat being created.

## Water Cooling

Air-cooled engines are easily recognisable by their noisier tone. The water-cooled engine is much quieter since the majority of engine noise is absorbed by the water jacketing around the parts of the engine which are subjected to combustion heat. Water is forced through the jackets under pressure from a pump. A supply of water is kept in the radiator placed in the best position for airflow cooling. When the car is stationary with the engine running, a fan ensures that air-flow is kept over the radiator.

As the engine warms up, it gives off its heat to the cool water in the jackets which then returns to the radiator where, after passing down the cooling tubes, it arrives, suitably cooled ready to be pumped back up to the water jackets.

As any motorist will tell you, possibly from bitter experience, the drawback of water cooling is that water freezes. Ice just will not circulate! Worse still, the frozen water takes up just under a tenth more space than unfrozen water. If antifreeze liquid is not put into the system, the first freeze up could severely damage the engine at the cylinder block, or the radiator.

Anti-freeze solutions give the water a lower freezing point (that is, it will take far colder weather than normal freezing point to have any possible effect on the water).

---

# Getting to know . . .

# DIESEL POWER

MANY VEHICLES ON the roads today use diesel fuel (gas oil). Most large commerical vehicles, lorries, buses and taxis etc., can gain a greater engine life and improved reliability due to the lower revving and greater size of the diesel unit.

## No Spark Plug

Diesel engines use a form of fuel injection — no spark plugs are used. The principle of diesel operation relies on the fact that the fuel has what is known as a low "flash point". The injectors do not mix the diesel with air as it is less easy to evaporate. Instead, *pure* air is drawn into the cylinder chamber through an inlet valve. The valve then closes as the piston rises compressing the air to approximately twice that of a petrol engine.

This rapid compression heats the air and just before the piston compresses the air to its maximum amount, diesel fuel is squirted into the combustion chamber where it "vaporises" in the hot, compressed air.

The heat in the combustion chamber naturally ignites the fuel, the mixture expands and so pushes the piston down the cylinder and onto its exhaust stroke when the burnt gases are expelled.

## Why choose diesel?

Why is the diesel engine favoured by taxi drivers, bus companies, long distance hauliers, and by the farmers who often prefer diesel-powered Land Rovers as farm workhorses? The advantages of this type of engine lie mainly in its reliability and long-lasting economies.

## . . . and why not?

Disadvantages however do exist — and would seem to outweigh the fuel economy, except when used on high mileage commercial vehicles. First, there is the minor point about the smell associated with a diesel engine. Second, the engine's increased weight over an equivalent petrol engine. Then there is the vibration caused by the less-even stroke of the diesel engine. The diesel engine is also slower on acceleration. But the main setback is the increased cost of building a diesel engine.

Diesel fuel for non-road use in farm machinery, boats, generators etc. has a red dye in it, so if it is used in a road vehicle the police can check whether full tax has been paid or not. (Agricultural diesel is about half the price of road-used diesel).

IT IS POSSIBLE to have a very straightforward and simple four-stroke cycle engine but unfortunately it would not be very practical for use in a car. The simplest form of four-stroke piston engine would be one with a single cylinder. This would use, needless to say, only one piston. But why impractical?

This single cylinder engine would unfortunately be rather deficient in the delivery of its power. Since it would have a single, relatively infrequent power stroke, the crankshaft (which we have seen, translates the piston's up-and-down motion into rotation) would receive an uneven turning effort. This turning effort, the power delivered, is technically known as "torque". Even twin-cylinder and four-cylinder engines can receive uneven torque, but the stabilising effect of the stored energy inherent in the flywheel assists in balancing this out as it is directly attached to the crankshaft.

## Two, Four, Six, Eight . . .

So to give any semblance of smooth running, at least two cylinders must be provided. But at low speeds, even the twin cylinder engine cannot give its best torque constantly.

The lowest number of cylinders needed to give acceptably smooth running is four. The crankshaft receives a regular power stroke via the pistons - with their power strokes following on one after the other.

Let's take a look at the cylinder layouts, and get to know about the strengths and weaknesses of each.

# Getting to know . . .
# ENGINE LAYOUTS

## "In-Line" Cylinder Engines

As the term implies, the cylinders are set in a line, one behind the other. Cars which use an in-line four-cylinder layout include the Ford Escort, the Morris and Austin 1100 and 1300's and Mini.

The evenly-spaced power strokes from the piston to the rotating motion of the crankshaft give acceptable comfort and freedom from undue vibration. And the height of the engine is not unduly limiting. Its slimness can assist the car designer.

Six cylinder in-line engines are smoother running than in-line fours.

There have been in-line eights (such as in some American saloons) but the engine length can only be accommodated under a lengthy bonnet. The long crankshaft also needs particularly good support.

## Horizontally-Opposed Four-Cylinder Engines

Here again, the term horizontally opposed refers to the relative positions of the cylinders. One pair of pistons lie horizontally in their cylinders to one side of the crankshaft, another pair to the other side.

Since the power stroke of one piston on one side of the horizontally opposed engine can be balanced by the power stroke of another piston on the opposite side, this low profile, compactly shaped form of layout has become popular for positioning at the rear of the vehicle and as such is often of the air-cooled type. The Volkswagen Beetle is an everyday example.

Long crankshafts take a tremendous strain, but the horizontally-opposed layout means that the shaft can be shorter, and so needs less support from main bearings.

This type of engine layout is often referred to as a "flat" four or "flat" six.

Six cylinder units, such as fitted into rear-engined Porsche cars, are expensive and, though smooth running, can be difficult to get at when servicing time comes round.

## "V"-engine layouts

The "V" layout has become quite a popular one today, especially in Ford cars. It is interesting to keep an eye out for, say, an early Corsair of about 1964 or 1965 — fitted with an in-line, four cylinder engine — and then to see a 1967 or 1968 model with its boot embellishment pronouncing to the world that under the bonnet there is a V4 layout.

Straight Four and Six Cylinder Layouts . . . Ford Escort 11/1300 etc, Mini, BLMC 11/1300, Chrysler Avenger, and Triumph 2000 (Straight Six).

Horizontally Opposed . . . as in Porsche (6-cyl.) V.W. (4 cylinder) etc.

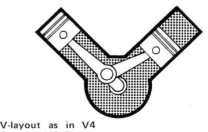

V-layout as in V4 Corsairs, V6 Capris, V8 Rovers, etc.

Most of the current BLMC (Austin and Morris) small car ranges have transversely-mounted, 4 cylinder in-line (or straight) engines driving the front wheels. On the left is an Austin 1300 saloon.

The V.W. Beetle range, including the 1974 V.W. 1303 here has air-cooled, horizontally-opposed engines fitted at the rear and driving the rear wheels. The 1303 also features self-stabilising steering which keeps the car on a straight course when braking.

A very sophisticated V-engine (left) from the Jaguar V12 layout (European specification) as used in the Series 3 E-type Jaguars.

Advantages of the V-engine layout include a shorter crankshaft than the straight form of engine; the overall engine size is smaller and of course slightly lower than the in-line unit.

A disadvantage crops up on the four-cylinder "V" formation. With no power strokes overlapping, some assistance is needed in the balancing of the engine. This means that an extra shaft which is weighted and geared down is set alongside the crankshaft.

However, six-cylinder versions do not require such a balancing trick to assist smooth running as the power strokes of the pistons do overlap.

## Smoother still

Even smoother is the 8-cylinder "V" engine layout where cylinders are v-eed (when looked at end-on) at 90 degrees. A V-6 engine will have an angle of about 60 degrees between the three cylinders on each side of the engine.

## Jaguar's 12-cylinders

The ultimate in V-layout must be the thirst V12 (yes, 12 cylinders) that Jaguar's fit to their luxurious V12 sports saloon. Even with the extensive use of light alloys (eg for the cylinder block) this monster tips the scales at 680 lbs - and that's without the gearbox! And imagine the complexity of a V-16 engined Ferrari model!!

# A CAR IS BORN

(See full text on page 9 through to page 21)

Preliminary Design: Every large manufacturer has a team of designers. From their "thought factories" come the cars of tomorrow.

Designs for future cars are first sculptured in clay. The brown model is to a 3/8-inch to 1 foot scale. Then full size models are produced in the clay medium.

When covered with a simulated paint finish, with silver foil for chrome work, the models are almost indistinguishable to the eye from the real thing.

Research into noise, vibration and mechanical efficiency (above) calls for trained personnel and up-to-the-minute machine-aids. Simulated road-tests under varying climatic conditions, windtunnel tests etc all give a feed-back of data. Improvements can then be made before cars are track-tested (below) and crash-tested (top right) to check safety features. A prototype car costs over £30,000 to build.

A sight to remember . . . moulten metal from the blast furnace. This will be used to make castings for engines and transmissions.

After automatic body welding, men spot weld other parts (left) before the car leaves to have other panels added.

Then, it's into a degreasing area and on to the paint dip. Primer coats follow, then a series of hand-applied top coats. Eventually painted, the body and the transmission, engine and suspension are mated (below). The car then moves along to be trimmed out, checked on the rolling road, and water-tested before delivery to the dispatch area.

## Getting to know . . .

# THE WANKEL ROTARY ENGINE

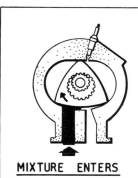

**MIXTURE ENTERS**

1 The rotor turns to uncover the inlet port and the petrol/air mixture is sucked in.

**MIXTURE COMPRESSED**

2 The rotor continues to turn and, because of the shape of the chamber and the rotor, the mixture is compressed.

**SPARK**

3 At the point of maximum compression a sparking plug fires the mixture and the expanding gases force the rotor round.

**EXHAUST**

4 At the conclusion of the cycle the exhaust port is uncovered and the gases are released.

FROM THE BEGINNING of the century engineers were intent on investigating the possibilities of an alternative to the conventional piston engine. British engineer Amplebey was one of the first to approach the problem of producing a "rotary" engine suitable for use in the vehicles of his time — around 1909. Several other attempts were to follow, but none seemed to challenge the technical supremacy and constant development of the reciprocating piston engine.

Not until the early 1950's, that is.

A German engineer, whose name is given to the Wankel rotary design, received great encouragement from the German NSU manufacturers. His design concept, improved over the years in line with research and improved technical knowledge and material treatments can now be seen under the bonnets of German NSU (R080) cars and Japanese Mazda saloons.

No other rotary design has challenged the Wankel. It was not, however, until 1964 that any serious production of the "revolutionary" competitor to the piston engine was contemplated.

## How the Wankel works . . .

The Wankel relies on a three sided (but not quite triangular) "rotor" which rolls around a geared central shaft. A casing with a regular, almost figure-of-eight, shaped to the interior contains the motor revolving on the fixed shaft. Because the toothed hole in the motor is larger than the geared shaft, the rotor's tips follow the figure of eight shaped in what is called an "eccentric" manner.

At any one time in the cycle all three tips are touching the inner surface of the casing, except when one may be just passing either a sparking plug, the fuel mixture inlet port, or the exhaust outlet.

### A similar "cycle" in the four-stroke principle

*The Wankel Rotary principle follows a similar cycle to the one we have seen displayed by the conventional four-stroke cycle.*

**Stage 1: Induction —** As we follow the course of one of the rotor tips, it starts moving clockwise around the casing and by so doing drags in the petrol and air mixture into the void or chamber created as the rotor moves around the casing

**Stage 2: Compression —** Our chosen rotor tip continues its eccentric journey following the shape of the casing — passing the sparking plug (possibly a twin plug arrangement). In doing so, the gas trapped in the void between this tip and the second tip finds itself being compressed. The rotor continues to compress the gas to the maximum and . . .

**Stage 3: Power —** The sparking plug (or plugs) come into action. The fuel mixture is ignited and on burning expands pushing the rotor round on its power stroke.

**Stage 4: Exhaust —** Our leading rotor tip is pushed round by the explosion and passes by the exhaust port, followed by the second rotor tip which, constantly in contact with the casing, shunts the exhaust gases away into the port.

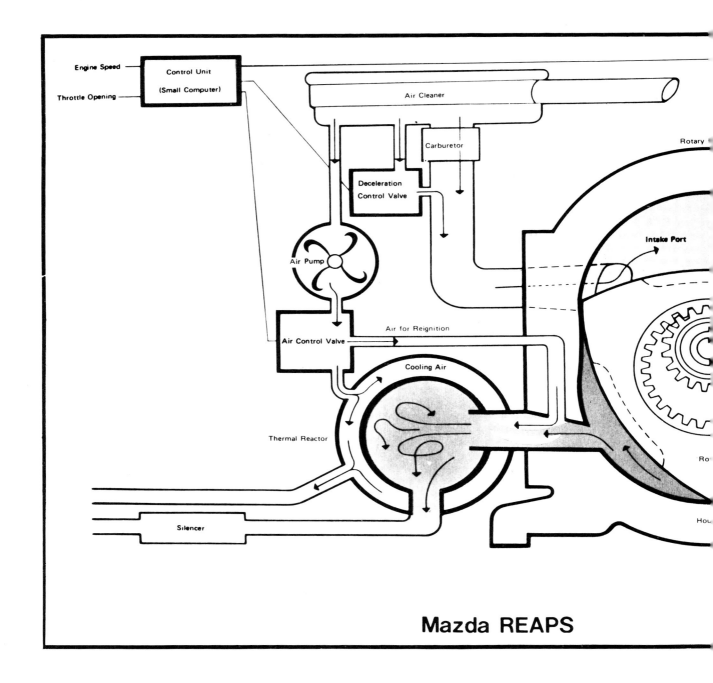

Engine Speed

Throttle Opening

Control Unit
(Small Computer)

Air Cleaner

Carburetor

Rotary

Deceleration
Control Valve

Intake Port

Air Pump

Air for Reignition

Air Control Valve

Cooling Air

Thermal Reactor

Ro

Silencer

Hou

**Mazda REAPS**

## What are the advantages of the rotary engine?

Going round and round is more efficient than the piston's going up, stopping (if only for a split second) and coming down . . . only to have to go back up again. Less energy is wasted.

The rotary design is very compact and allows the engine to take up less room in the engine compartment which can also take a lower profile. A designer's dream come true.

The system is very light as there are far fewer parts — and more important far fewer *moving* parts to wear out, distort, or fail.

Otherwise, there is only one possible drawback. The rotor tips obviously need to be constantly in contact with the wall of the casing and be thoroughly "gas tight". The tips and the casing therefore need to be able to stand up to such wear.

38

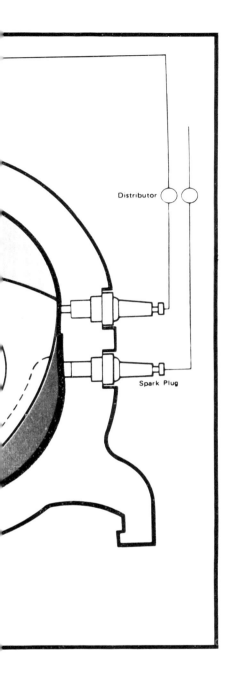

IN THE USA the Environmental Protection Agency demanded of car manufacturers that vehicles sold as of the year 1975 meet their strict controls on exhaust emission. In the verbal battle that followed the US manufacturers managed to win round one by finally getting agreement from the EPA to delay the controls for a further year. They have already spent hundreds of millions of dollars in trying to develop 'clean' production engines, but could still not guarantee to meet the 1975 regulations, let alone the even more stringent proposed 1976 regulations.

Mazda REAPS consists basically of a thermal reactor which reburns carbon monoxide and hydrocarbons, a computer which is programmed to control the reactor, an exhaust gas purification control device and a blow-by gas recirculation device. Even with all of this equipment built-in to the car only a minimal adverse affect on the performance or driving operation was claimed.

The exhaust gas recirculation device which completes the operation is said to reduce exhaust emission to a very low level.

In a few years time traffic will no longer be allowed to pollute the atmosphere with harmful chemicals; it is Mazda's proud boast that they were the first to take up the guantlet on environmental protection and turn it into a reality for the good of all living things.

But other contenders to the anti-pollution war may prove more efficient, less difficult to manufacture, and be suitable for operation on fuels other than petrol.

High performance cars can use two rotors set in phase to each other to provide a really lightweight and efficient power source. Though most saloon cars use carburration in order to deliver the fuel-air mixture, petrol injection is possible and yet again boosts the potential power.

If you would like to learn more about the Wankel Rotary engine, ask any NSU or Mazda car agent for their very informative brochures.

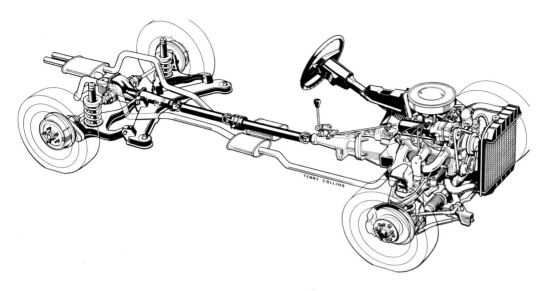

Getting to know . . .

# TRANSMISSION SYSTEMS

OUR CAR ENGINE is a pretty efficient piece of engineering. Small and compact as it is, it packs a lot of torque (or turning effort). But how on earth does an engine transmit the power it makes from, say, under the bonnet to the rear wheels. This type of system is the most commonly used — front engine, rear-wheel drive.

The rear end of an engine houses the flywheel, a heavy carefully balanced mass fitted behind the crankshaft. The flywheel's momentum, as we have already seen, helps to balance any uneven motion caused by the engine's power strokes.

All around the circumference of the flywheel are teeth into which the starter motor engages, when the ignition key is turned in the dashboard.

So, a turn of the key, and the flywheel is spun by the starter motor, and hopefully, our car engine springs to life.

If a long piece of round metal, a propeller shaft as we might call it, was attached to the flywheel, it too would rotate and its rotation could be translated, by some means, across the car to join up with the rear wheels.

If this were done, then the car would pull away immediately on starting up which would not really do. Also, the propeller shaft would only turn at one maximum speed — giving us the equivalent of a single gear with which to cope with the high torque need to move off, the torque to climb hills, and also be able to cope with varying speeds on the flat.

## The clutch

To solve the problem of instant movement on starting the engine, a clutch is inserted into the transmission line-up. This enables the driver, at the press of a foot pedal, to disengage the clutch from the flywheel and so cut off all power transmission to the propeller shaft.

The modern diaphragm clutch contains a special "plate" which is connected to a "speed selector box" — a gearbox.

## The gearbox

If you have ever ridden a bike up a hill and used gears to enable you progressively to change from a high gear (for cruising along the flat, say) to a lower gear, and possibly a lower one still near the brow of the hill, you will know how useful the bike's "gearbox" can be. It enables you to cope with most situations without tiring your body — which is the equivalent of the car's engine, your legs being like pistons transmitting a "two-stoke" effect.

The same idea has to be arranged for the car. A low high-torque gear for moving off up to a certain speed, or number of suitable engine revolutions, is needed first. This may be fine for accelerating up to about 5 to 10 miles per hour. Then a second gear must come into play to cope with the next engine revolution to power situation — so the driver disengages the clutch to cut off power from the flywheel and then slips the gear lever into second gear.

# HOW THE GEARBOX WORKS...

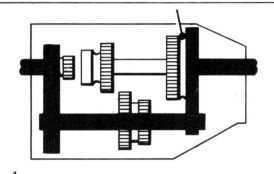

**1.**

FIRST GEAR. The highest ratio of engine speed to transmission speed to provide maximum power at the driving wheels.

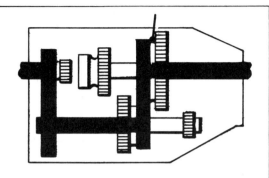

**2**

SECOND GEAR. Synchromesh clutches dis-engage first gear and engage second gear.

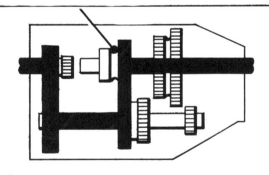

**3**

THIRD GEAR. This ratio employs the last combination of gears between the mainshaft and the layshaft.

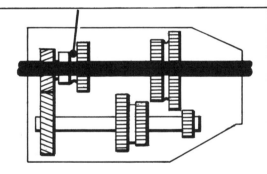

**4**

FOURTH OR TOP GEAR. All clutches are released except those on the mainshaft which lock-up to give 'direct drive'.

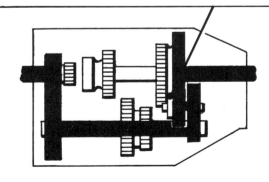

**R**

REVERSE. An extra gear wheel is inserted into the first gear set-up to reverse the direction of rotation.

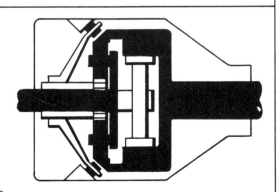

**O**

OVERDRIVE. Placed between the gearbox and the final drive it provides an extra high ratio to improve cruising economy.

This special Land Rover "all terrain" vehicle has a somewhat intricate transmission compared with the family saloon!

Speed is increasing as the driver moves faster and faster away on the flat. So third gear will then be arranged by the movement of the gear lever to the next position. We're probably doing about 25 miles per hour now — much more and the engine's revs will start telling us that they are doing overtime.

So into fourth, and so on most cars, final forward gearing to build up speed even further as the driver presses his foot on the accelerator pedal.

Up comes a hill, and it's back to third gear initially — otherwise the load imposed on the engine by trying to push a considerable mass up a steep hill will cause the engine to labour. The driver presses the clutch in to disengage the flywheel and follows this by choosing third gear and then bringing the clutch back into play to maintain it.

And so on down to second gear and, at about fast walking speed, right down to first using the clutch each time between changes. Most modern cars have "Synchromesh" incorporated which synchronises the meshing speeds of connecting cogs. A bad gear change, or lack of synchromesh shows by giving a crashing sound.

Traffic lights ahead? On red? As he is waiting in the traffic queue for the green "go" light, a driver will apply the handbrake to stop the car rolling back (or being pushed forward) and select "neutral" which disengages the gearbox and allows the engine to "idle" without fuss.

Another gear, reverse, is provided so that the driver can drive the car backwards into his garage, or manoeuvre into a parking space.

## Overdrive

Some cars, mainly large saloons and sports cars, are fitted with a fifth gear which can be selected to provide economical high-speed cruising without putting unnecessary strain on the engine. Overdrive, then, is the equivalent of a fifth gear.

## Automatic Gearboxes

One of the smoothest ways to drive is with an automatic transmission which not only changes gear smoothly and at the correct engine revs. but also saves anything like 500 gear changes for a motorist trying to inch his way through a mile or so of London's roads.

Most cars with automatic transmission have the fact stamped all over their boot lids and have a gear selector which often reads PRND21. These letters stand for Park; Reverse; Neutral; Drive (the position for fully automatic engine selection) and figures 1 and 2 which indicated that the driver can select either first or second gear manually for quicker acceleration before sliding the gear selector into auto-drive.

Also useful for the automatic transmission owner is the facility to get "kick down". This makes overtaking a safer, more speedy operation by limiting the throttle pedal travel to a point past which next the lowest gear is automatically chosen.

## Keeping the transmission in line — "diffs"

There are now many vehicles which have front-mounted engines driving the two front wheels — "front wheel drive" cars such as Mini, 1100 and BLMC 1300 models to name but a few. The engine can run along the centre line of the car, or across the car ("transversely" as with the cars mentioned).

In such circumstances as these, the engine, gearbox and front axle are combined as one unit. The transverse engine uses "drive shafts" to keep constant drive to the wheels and special joints to look after varying angles of wheel turn when under way.

## FRONT ENGINE — REAR WHEEL DRIVE

## FRONT ENGINE — FRONT WHEEL DRIVE

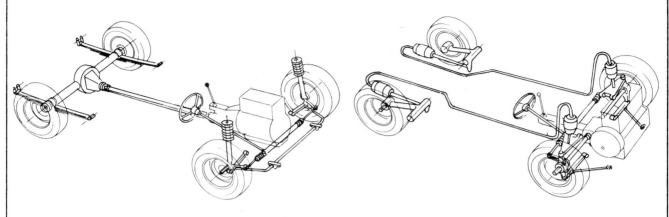

The most common type of layout used on family saloons. It uses independent front suspension with engine and gearbox to front and a propeller shaft transmitting the power to the rear wheels via a "live" rear axle. The rear axle is a solid tube mounted on half-eliptic springs. The front suspension is of the MacPherson strut design (similar to that used on Ford Escort and Cortina).

This layout saves the use of a prop shaft and rigid rear axle. The engine is mounted transversly. The Gearbox is under the engine transmitting power to the front wheels via drive shafts and "constant velocity" joints. These allow the wheels to turn and the drive shaft to bend all at once. Damping is by rubber springs interconnected with a fluid suspension medium (BLMC Hydrolastic suspension). As fitted to Minis, 1110, 1300 etc.

## REAR ENGINE — REAR WHEEL DRIVE

## FRONT ENGINE — REAR WHEEL DRIVE

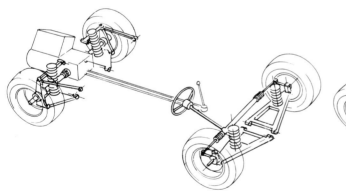
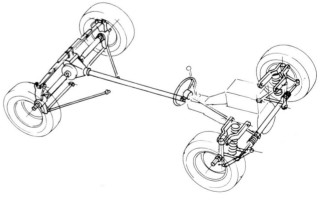

This layout is used to keep the engine behind the driver and passengers. The front suspension is independent and could be of various types. Shown above is the swinging half axle. The engine transmits power forward to a gearbox, then to the rear wheels. (Chrysler Imps, Porsche, V.W. Beetle etc.)

This system has 4-wheel independent suspension but has engine in front driving the rear wheels. The independent rear suspension is used to give a more comfortable ride and costs more to produce. The rear springing shown is transverse leaf type but coil springs and torsion bars could be used. (As in Triumph Herald. Also Jaguar, Ford Granada, Rolls Royce, BMW etc. with different suspension systems).

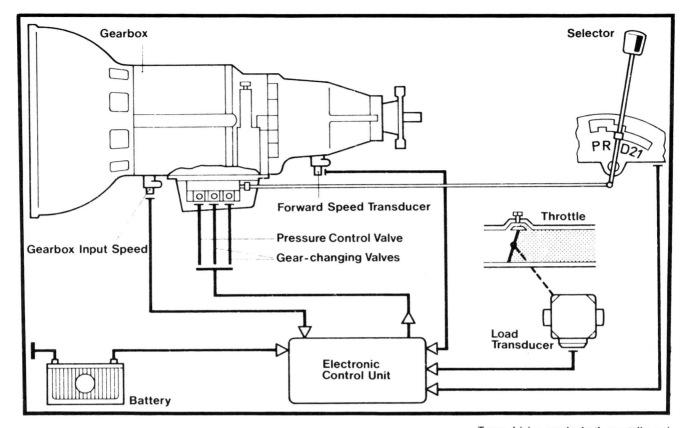

Labels in figure:
Gearbox
Selector
PR D21
Forward Speed Transducer
Pressure Control Valve
Gear-changing Valves
Gearbox Input Speed
Throttle
Load Transducer
Electronic Control Unit
Battery

## Belt up!

One of the first methods used to transmit power from the engine to the rear wheels was by the use of a long belt which ran directly from the engine to a pulley fitted to the rear wheels' axle.

Old as the idea may be (and inefficient as it might have been in the early days of motoring!) a similar idea is used by the nifty little Daf cars which come from Holland.

The belt-drive system as used in Daf's fully automatic cars comprises two parallel toothed belts which are stretched from pulleys each side of a gearbox unit to pulleys on the rear axle.

Simple, but effective, the Daf's Variomatic system is a very flexible one where the car's speed adjusts pulley diameters and the driver's throttle pressure affects a vacuum chamber. These two points, taken together, affect the gear chosen by the automatic gearbox.

## All wheels — go!

Can all four wheels be driving wheels?

There have been several four-wheel drive cars which have been brought onto the market — as well as the well-known workhorse, the Landrover which can be supplied in four-wheel drive form.

What are the advantages of four-wheel drive?

If all four wheels are driven, a car's tyres can exert far

Town driving can be both mentally and physically tiring. Though automatic gearboxes can absorb as much as 30 or 40 per cent of an engine's power (and hence increase fuel consumption) this Bosch electronically controlled 3-speed transmission should ease strains on both engine and driver.

more grip on rough ground, and especially on slippery surfaces, as the whole weight of the vehicle can be used to assist what engineers call traction.

On made-up roads Land Rovers can revert to rear-wheel drive for economy and practicability. But some saloon cars such as the Jensen FF (the FF stands for Ferguson Formula) have been successfully fitted with full four-wheel drive transmission.

What goes up — Must come down!

# Getting to know . . .
# Suspension & Steering

ALTHOUGH THERE ARE various ways and means of coupling suspension systems, they all basically rely on a spring and a shock absorber. When the wheel hits a bump in the road the spring is compressed so that the car can travel reasonably evenly over the top without a jarring thud. In being compressed the spring takes in energy.

As the spring is compressed, so is the shock absorber, and the spring is compelled to use the energy it initially took in to extend the shock absorber, which is designed to oppose the spring. This is how the car is saved from

45

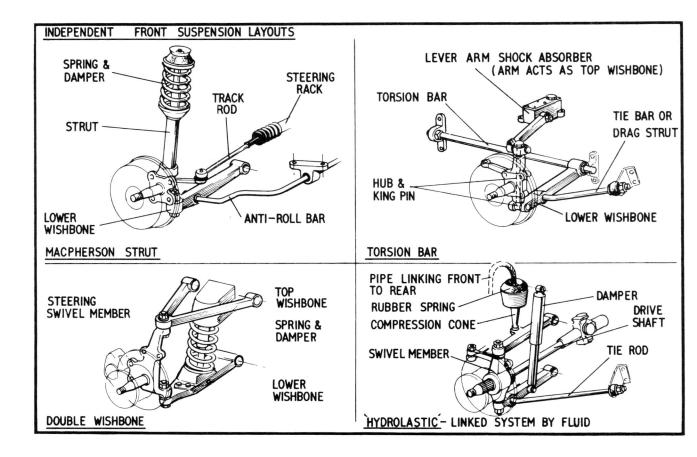

INDEPENDENT FRONT SUSPENSION LAYOUTS

SPRING & DAMPER
STEERING RACK
TRACK ROD
STRUT
LOWER WISHBONE
ANTI-ROLL BAR

MACPHERSON STRUT

LEVER ARM SHOCK ABSORBER (ARM ACTS AS TOP WISHBONE)
TORSION BAR
TIE BAR OR DRAG STRUT
HUB & KING PIN
LOWER WISHBONE

TORSION BAR

STEERING SWIVEL MEMBER
TOP WISHBONE
SPRING & DAMPER
LOWER WISHBONE

DOUBLE WISHBONE

PIPE LINKING FRONT TO REAR
RUBBER SPRING
COMPRESSION CONE
SWIVEL MEMBER
DAMPER
DRIVE SHAFT
TIE ROD

HYDROLASTIC - LINKED SYSTEM BY FLUID

the majority of road bumps, the spring taking in the energy and the shock absorber getting rid of it.

The job of the shock absorber is to prevent all sorts of unwanted movement such as body roll on corners, and pitching due to acceleration and braking. The shock absorber is the most important part of the suspension as far as control is concerned. Once it becomes worn and does not offer sufficient resistance to movement the springs become insufficiently damped and the body is free to make unwanted movement. The car pitches nose down under braking, lightening the load on the rear wheels so that they lock. This will cause the car to skid on a bad surface and reduce braking efficiency considerably on a good surface.

Similarly, if cornering forces are allowed to cause excessive body roll this will make driving at what should be normal speeds untidy at best and could well be unsafe.

The steering and suspension system carry the complete control system and should be given very careful attention by the owner of a car. Wear in the steering and/or suspension joints allows the wheels to wander from where they should be! This gives woolly, imprecise steering with a lot of lost motion at the wheel,

Ford Cortina front suspension and steering gear (above) and rear suspension (right) with anti-roll bar.

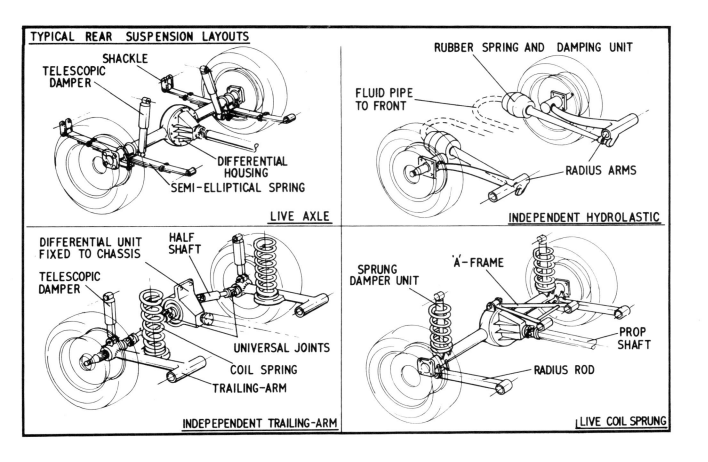

TYPICAL REAR SUSPENSION LAYOUTS

SHACKLE
TELESCOPIC DAMPER
DIFFERENTIAL HOUSING
SEMI-ELLIPTICAL SPRING

LIVE AXLE

RUBBER SPRING AND DAMPING UNIT
FLUID PIPE TO FRONT
RADIUS ARMS

INDEPENDENT HYDROLASTIC

DIFFERENTIAL UNIT FIXED TO CHASSIS
HALF SHAFT
TELESCOPIC DAMPER
UNIVERSAL JOINTS
COIL SPRING
TRAILING-ARM

INDEPEPENDENT TRAILING-ARM

SPRUNG DAMPER UNIT
'A'-FRAME
PROP SHAFT
RADIUS ROD

LIVE COIL SPRUNG

causing snatchy brake action which will pull the car away from a straight line. This is unsafe as you never really know what the car is going to do next!

The other bad effect of wear in the suspension and steering joints is accelerated tyre wear. Sloppy or badly aligned steering can easily halve the effective life of a tyre.

## All gassed up — Hydragas suspension

A car suspension designer who is asked to design a car that has both an easy ride and good handling finds himself trying to bring together two contradictory objectives: traditionally, the softer the ride, the worse the handling; the better the handling, the harsher the ride. The problem is particularly difficult in small, lively family saloons.

Hydragas, a second generation of interconnected suspension developed from the Hydrolastic system, is one answer of great simplicity. It goes a long way towards reconciling this conflict of requirements, giving "big car" ride with superlative handling.

Designed by Moulton Developments Limited in conjunction with Austin Morris Group, Hydragas is

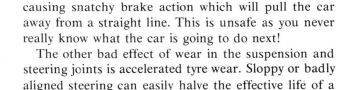

*All gassed up . . .*
*Allegro's suspension system*

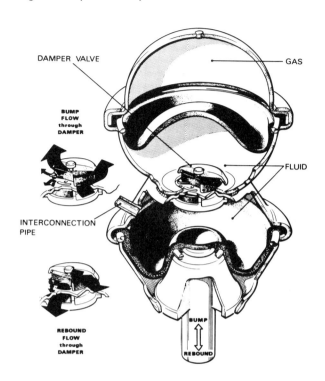

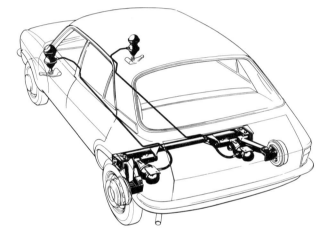

manufactured by the Dunlop Company. It is fitted to the Austin Allegro frontwheel-drive, transverse-engined range.

Hydragas suspension comprises an integral spring and damper unit at each wheel. The units use a sealed-for-life inert gas as a springing medium. The weight of the car is carried by water-based fluid under pressure and the units are interconnected front to rear.

Hydragas damping is designed to last the life of the car and the spring-damper unit requires no maintenance. Its unique arrangement of using a rolling diaphragm eliminates the friction and wear of sliding seals.

The Hydragas unit is a nitrogen-filled spherical chamber welded on to the top of a displacer chamber. Between these two chambers are carefully shaped holes covered by rubber compression blocks to control the flow of fluid between the upper and lower chamber. This valve is a two-way device and provides the required suspension damping.

The displacer chamber is hermetically sealed at its lower end by a rubber diaphragm which rolls between the skirt and the piston in response to wheel movement.

The gas provides the springing and is sealed for life.

# Getting to know . . .

# WHEELS and TYRES

by Ken Roud of Dunlop

WHY DO WE have pneumatic rubber tyres on our cars, bikes and lorries — even wheelbarrows? There are a number of reasons, the main ones being grip on the road, safety, comfort and the long life offered by a tyre.

As most tyres are used on cars and all new ideas were for improvement on this kind of tyre it is best that we concentrate on these. But before doing so we should have some idea of how they came into being.

## History of the Wheel and Tyre

The use of the wheel, as we know, goes back very far in history, and this, as every schoolboy worth his salt should know, was at least 5,000 years ago. At first they were only wooden discs but as time passed they became spoked wheels which meant wheels were lighter, and consequently could be made much larger.

Despite improvements in the design and construction, these wheels still had to run on solid rims — which meant that they gave a very bumpy ride. They often became cracked and eventually broke. But they existed right up to the end of the last century with the discomfort at least partially overcome by the use of various kinds of springs on carriages themselves.

It is interesting to note that it wasn't until pretty late in the 19th century, with the development of mechanical power and better roads, that wheel design improved tremendously. About 15,000 patents for wheels were taken out during the years between 1855 and 1930!

A number of very important discoveries and inventions came about during the 1880's which really started the wheels rolling, as one might say! For a start, in 1839 an American, Charles Goodyear, discovered that by heating natural rubber together with sulphur he produced a material that was relatively tough, durable and which was not affected by the weather. This discovery was also made by an Englishman, Thomas Hancock, in 1843.

So now we had the raw material for tyres but even then the *pneumatic* tyre had not yet been invented. This came about in 1888 when John Boyd Dunlop became concerned over his son Johnny's health. He knew from his own experience travelling around Belfast as a veterinary surgeon that the continuous jolting received in travelling was harmful. He thus started to experiment by buying materials from a local chemist and building a "prototype" tyre fitted to a solid wooden disc. When bowled like a hoop in competition with a solid rubber tyred wheel it rolled farther and faster.

Encouraged by the result Dunlop made more tubes from sheet rubber, covered them with canvas and fitted them to wooden rims. These he tried out on his son's tricycle and they were so successful that in July 1888 he took out a patent. Quite unknown to him a pneumatic tyre had been developed and patented by R.W. Thompson as early as 1845, but the idea attracted so little attention that Thompson's was soon forgotten.

The Dunlop tyre had its first public trial in 1889. This was at a Queen's College event, Belfast, where they were fitted to a bicycle competing in the cycle racing events. There were jeers from the crowd who called out "pudding wheels" and "sausage tyres". There jeers soon turned to amazement, however, as the rider of the cycle, William Hume, won easily. The new tyres were both smoother and faster.

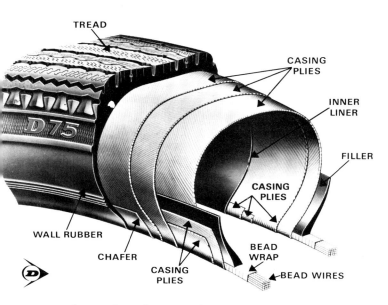

A crossply tyre's construction used today — but based on principles established many years ago.

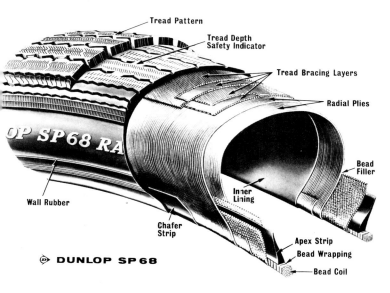

Construction of a radial tyre shows how the carcass is built up.

## Development of the Tyre

Following the success of this "original" tyre a company was formed under the name of The Pneumatic Tyre and Booth Cycle Agency. The first Dunlop tyres fitted to a bicycle employed "Gent's Yacht Sail Cloth" for the textile portion which was used to prevent the inner tube bursting. This material was probably made of cotton, or perhaps linen or flax. In any case it was a fibre of natural origin. Today, synthetic fibres or fine steel wire are used and during the time that Dunlop has been making tyres they have examined every known type of fibre with a view to its possible use.

The original choice of sail cloth was a good one as it was strong, not too expensive and readily available. A few years later the inventor was using a specially woven linen cloth produced for him by a Scottish textile mill. In the beginning the cloth was covered with a layer of rubber to provide a longer lasting cover material and to give better grip.

Thus began the humble progress of the tyre industry and the highly specialised art of tyre technology.

The earliest motor vehicle tyres were made from square woven canvas until about the time of the 1914-18 war when certain American manufacturers and the Palmer Company in England began to use a construction in which a single, fairly thick strand of rubberised cotton cord was wound backwards and forwards across a suitable former, so that in effect successive "plies" of rubberised unwoven fabric were built up. This was known as the "Palmer Cord" process and performance-wise it had many advantages over the older woven canvas. Dunlop used this process for some time but eventually reverted to a modified version of the unwoven fabric used for cycle tyres. This led to further improved tyre performance plus simpler techniques in production.

Coupled with the developments in textiles was the gradual improvement in the quality of the rubbers used. Just after the turn of the century it was discovered that various fillers, oxides, etc., improved the life of the rubber, gave better grip, and also accelerated the manufacturing process. By the time of the 1914-18 war, rubber development was relatively well ahead. Synthetic rubbers reared their heads at about this time and were first used in Germany for tyres but only as an emergency measure.

Between the war years no startling developments occurred but progress and development went forward at a steady pace. Better and better rubber compounds were produced as were the textiles used in the casing. Demands by the ever-expanding car industry also helped to push along developments. Special requirements such as World Speed Attempts and car racing speeded up the rate of technological innovation.

By the beginning of the second World War, tyre construction was basically of the one type, the now familiar and conventional "cross-ply" tyre. The big step forward came during the war when synthetic rubber began to play a larger part in the compounding for tyre treads. This development meant the provision of tyres that gave better grip and also longer life. Today most tread compounds incorporate a synthetic developed specifically for the tyre's ultimate use. However, natural rubber is still preferred for the casing as it can absorb greater flexing and heat generation.

Following the development of the more sophisticated synthetic rubbers the next significant and important step forward in tyre design was the advent of the "radial" tyre. This was first introduced by Michelin who completed their development in 1948 and introduced the first radial tyre to the public as long ago as 1949.

Dunlop, Pirelli and other European tyre manufacturers were soon to follow suit. However, whereas Michelin concentrated on steel plies, the other manufacturers opted for synthetic fibre plies. The trend today is to use a mixture of steel and synthetic fibre, and one manufacturer has recently developed a tyre incorporating fine glass fibre plies.

Most of the major tyre manufacturers have very useful booklets available to young people wishing to find out more about tyre technology and manufacture. Drop them a line, and ask what is available.

## Cross Ply? Or Radial?

The cross-ply tyre, as made basically for the past 50 years, is built up of a number of layers of cord fabric, virtually weftless in structure. The treads cross the centreline of the tyre at an approximate angle of 35 degrees.

The radial, however, has a casing made up of plies, the cords of which cross the centreline of the tyre at 90 degrees, so that they run like horseshoes. On the top of this casing is a rigid belt or breaker comprising several plies that run round the tyre with the cords at a slight angle.

Although the modern cross-ply tyre gives an excellent ride and a fair mileage the radial, because of its flexibility and larger spread of tread area on contact, can in many instances give up to 80-100 per cent more mileage.

Because of the increased flexibility a radial also allows steering to be more precise, and as is often said, a car fitted with radials appears to "run on rails".

Cross-ply tyres are still being produced in large quantities and are being specified as original equipment by many European car manufacturers. However, over the past few years new models have been designed specifically for radial fitment only and it is anticipated that within a few more years up to 80 per cent of the vehicles on the road will be shod with radials. The main market for cross-ply tyres will be in the replacement area for cars that are not designed for or are not suitable for radial fitment.

## Recognising Tyres

Not all tyres for cars are the same. To begin with of course, there are the two types, cross-ply and radial. So, how can a motorist tell the difference?

A cross-ply tyre is thinner across the tyre and when on a car, the part on the road does not spread very much. With a radial however, it looks fatter and bulges where the tyre contacts the road, and with some makes they even appear as if the tyre is almost flat!

The tread pattern on a cross-ply appears to be much closer and heavier than on a radial. With a little experience it is easy to tell the difference but to tell the size and how fast it can run, it is necessary to investigate further.

Tyre sizes are based on the width of the tyre when inflated and the diameter of the rim of the wheel to which it is fitted. For example a car tyre that is called a 5.20-10 means that it is 5.20 inches wide *overall* (not just the tread) and that it sits on a rim diameter of 10 inches. This method of sizing also applied to lorry and truck tyres and is accepted throughout the world as the standard way of sizing tyres.

Today, this information is made more complicated by the addition of other figures and letters.

Radial tyres are usually shown in millimetres but their diameter may be in inches, e.g. 165-15. In some cases both may be in millimetres such as 135-355.

Now we add a coding for the type of tyre!

Cross-ply tyres are not normally coded but radials are and this is shown by adding on "R" to the figures to give a more complete coding, e.g. 165-R-13.

There is one more item to be added which refers to speed and is an indication of how fast the tyre should be run. Three letters are used; "S" for speed which is for about 65-70 miles per hour, "H" for high speed for about 95-100 miles per hour and "V" for very high speed which is up to about 130-140 miles per hour. Thus we now have the full coding — an example of a cross-ply: 5.50-S-12; and a radial: 185-HR-13.

# Safety Round-up

The Rover 2000 and Mini 1275GT were the first cars to have the Dunlop Denovo Failsafe (Total Mobility) tyre and wheel offered as an option.

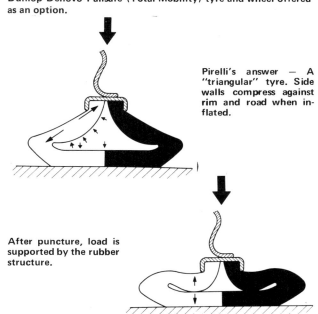

Pirelli's answer — A "triangular" tyre. Side walls compress against rim and road when inflated.

After puncture, load is supported by the rubber structure.

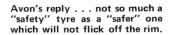

Avon's reply . . . not so much a "safety" tyre as a "safer" one which will not flick off the rim.

EVERY CAR on our roads must have brakes by law. Just imagine the situation if cars did not have brakes fitted! True, the engine can be used to "brake" a car in an emergency, or merely for convenience, such as choosing the braking effect of third or even second gear when descending a steep hill. When motoring in Devon, Cornwall and Scotland a motorist will notice many signs denoting a red surround to a white triangle picturing a representation of a hill in black with supplementary information about the gradient, such as 1 in 4, or 1 in 6. Of these two examples, the 1 in 4 gradient will be the steeper — about the steepest a car is able to ascend and descend in safety in good conditions.

The engine will only provide some "braking" effort by holding engine speed back by using the low gearing of the transmission. The foot-brake will have to be used in order to bring the car to a complete halt, or to control the car on sharp bends.

There are various types of braking systems fitted to the many car designs seen on our roads.

Even before the First World War (1914-18) some racing cars were fitted with what are known as "internal expanding brakes" — a metal band fitted with friction material which was forced outwards to come into contact with a drum. By slowing down the drum, the wheels themselves were slowed and eventually brought (hopefully) to a stop. Such systems were regarded as a great improvement on the very earliest methods which often resembled a cart's braking system — a wheel which the driver rotated so screwing down a curved wooden

Rover 2000 is fitted with servo-assisted brakes.

Girling hydraulic front brake.

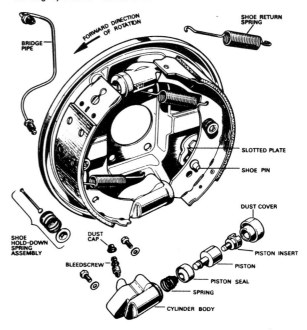

block onto the rear road wheels' rims!

The internal expanding brake became more popular during the 1920's and though development has one apace since those early days, the systems used still have some semblance to those we have fitted to cars today.

The next logical development, encouraged by research for improved braking systems for war-time vehicles, came about in the early 1930's when cars were appearing in America with "hydraulically-operated brakes".

## Hydraulic Brakes

Liquids are difficult to compress and this fact is used in hydraulic brake operation. If pressure is appl_ d to a

operated by the slave cylinder's piston or pistons.

Now, however, drum brakes are being superseded by the very efficient disc brake . . .

## Disc Brakes

A disc brake, though more exposed to the elements than a drum brake, finds this an advantage in that the heat build-up when braking is more easily expended. In this way they provide better performance by not overheating and causing the brakes to "fade" or lose their effectiveness.

A disc brake is made up of a solid cast iron disc which rotates with the car's wheel to which it is attached. Its

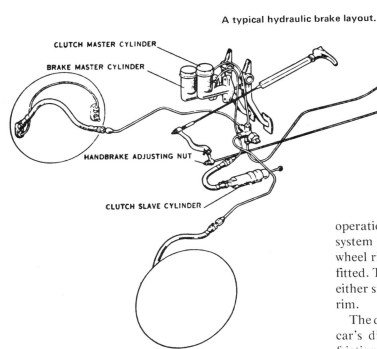

A typical hydraulic brake layout.

CLUTCH MASTER CYLINDER

BRAKE MASTER CYLINDER

HANDBRAKE COMPENSATOR

HANDBRAKE ADJUSTING NUT

CLUTCH SLAVE CYLINDER

operation is similar to that of a bicycle's caliper brake system where a caliper arches each side of the bike's wheel rim and provides a place for a brake block to be fitted. The caliper when operated causes the brake pads either side of the rim to come inwards and pinch on the rim.

The difference between a bicycle's caliper brake and a car's disc brake is that the car's system involves the friction pads pinching on a large metal disc which is attached to the wheel. As the friction slows the disc's rotation, it must slow the wheel as well.

## Tough work . . .

Everyone, these days, wants to save himself as much hard work as possible. Even braking can call for no small amount of energy to be given by a driver. In order to keep pressure on the footbrake to a minimum yet ensure that braking effect is maximised, some manufacturers fit their cars with servo-assisted brake systems, a system which basically makes use of the vacuum created by an engine to help apply the brakes.

If the servo-assistance mechanism fails for any reason the driver can (fortunately) still apply the brakes, but will need to put far more pressure on the brake pedal.

suitable liquid or brake fluid, then the power will be transmitted throughout the fluid's system which involves pipelines to the braking gear at each wheel.

The fluid is brought under pressure by the driver pressing his foot on the footbrake. This places the fluid in a master cylinder under pressure and this is felt by individual "slave" cylinders fitted to each brake area.

The slave cylinders have small pistons inside them and as the fluid pressure builds up, the pistons push outwards forcing friction pads against the brake drum. The drum is attached to the wheel and revolves with it. Friction to slow the drum (and hence the wheel) is supplied by brake "shoes" lined with hard-wearing friction material. The shoes are the parts that are

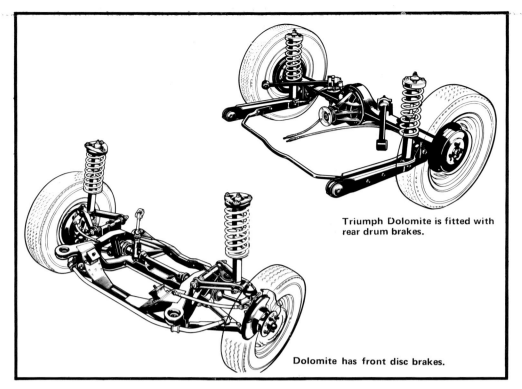

Triumph Dolomite is fitted with rear drum brakes.

Dolomite has front disc brakes.

## Just in case

Loss of brake fluid from the system is like loss of blood to a human. But, unlike the human's heart, a car without brakes will carry on under momentum! In order to give a greater degree of safety to the braking system, some of the more expensive car ranges (and in recent years, some of the less expensive ones too) are being provided with a dual-circuit hydraulic fluid system.

Such "fail-safe" systems incorporate two independent hydraulic circuits to either just the front brakes, or to front and one rear brake. It is estimated that with only the two front brakes operational, braking efficiency is approximately 60 per cent. The three-wheel fail-safe system would give approximately 80 per cent of the car's normal braking capacity.

## Handbrake — so very handy

If all else fails, the driver always has the handbrake to fall back on. The handbrake, normally associated with parking the car, or preventing the vehicle from rolling forward or backwards while waiting in traffic, is also a valuable piece of emergency equipment.

Most modern cars rely on the handbrake operating only the rear wheels brakes. This is done (and is required by law to be done) by some mechanical means such as metal rods, or wire cables — a system quite divorced from that of the foot brake. There are various methods of linkages, but no matter which is used the handbrake is one of the most important parts of a car's equipment which any driver would be wise to keep in good repair.

## Getting to know . . .

# A CAR'S ELECTRICS

A CAR'S ELECTRICAL system is often held in awe by many motorists but perhaps, if we take a look at the ignition system and then other electrical apparatus, we may be able to understand things a little better. We have seen, for example, how the engine's cylinders take in a mixture of petrol and air which has to be ignited to push the piston down the cylinder and so help to produce power which can be transmitted to the transmission. But how does the sparking plug in each cylinder gets its ignition spark?

## The ignition system

Everythings starts at the battery. A car's battery is a much neglected part of the vehicle's anatomy — only missed on a cold winter's day when the driver finds that the turn of the ignition key brings only a dull throb intimating that the battery is in need of recharging.

A battery is made up of various "cells" each separated from the next to prevent an electrical short-circuit. Each cell comprises negative and positive electrodes immersed in a chemical solution — sulphuric acid is used as the "electrolyte". As the battery is used, the electrolyte level tends to drop and distilled water has to be fed into the battery to "top up" the level. When, at some stage, the battery's charge gets too low for efficient operation, the electrolyte has to be regenerated by passing an electrical current through the electrode plates which also improves their efficiency. Each cell's plate system can offer approximately two volts of electrical power so a 12-volt car system will have a battery containing six cells. Some cars work off a 6-volt system but this mainly applies to a few European and some older American cars.

The battery is the heart of the car's electrical power needed to "turn the engine over". When the motorist puts the car's ignition key in position, and then turns it to "on" power flows from the battery to a "coil" whose job in life is to take the battery's 12 volt power and boost it. This is done by feeding the 12 volt charge around a coil of wire known as a "primary winding". Nothing much happens until the flow is interrupted momentarily when rapid changes in the magnetic fields inside the coil induce an extremely high voltage into a series of tighter windings positioned inside the first set. A contact-breaker is the item which creates the momentary interruption to the electrical flow.

A very heavy cable carries the coil's high voltage (boosted from 12 to 8 to 10,000 volts) to the distributor. The distributor does three jobs. It houses the contact breaker which interrupts the electrical flow in the coil, and then distributes the high voltage to the correct cylinder at the correct time. This is done by the rotor arm which rotates feeding the power to each of the spark plug leads in turn.

The next cylinder to require a spark for ignition is fed the power required to the cylinder's spark plug. The current travels down the sparking plug's high tension lead, through the terminal at the top of the plug, and then down the centre of the electrode which is covered with a special insulator to prevent even the slightest leakage of electricity.

The electrode runs out of the bottom of the plug — so the high voltage current follows until it reaches the end where it "jumps" across to another electrode. This produces the high-power spark which ignites the fuel mixture.

The steps recently made in improving car ignition systems have meant that some cars are now being fitted with a form of transistorised system. Joseph Lucas, the Bosch company, and others are now offering systems which have come about from the sporting front. The conventional ignition system may be able to produce about 24,000 sparks every minute but racing machines, sometimes with many more cylinders to fire than the average motorist dare dream of, need in excess of 70,000

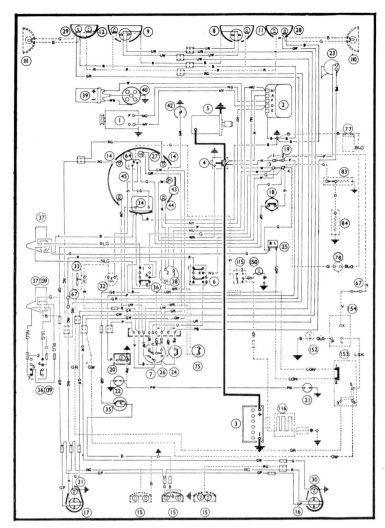

**A typical wiring diagram**

sparks each minute. The ultimate in transistorised or electronic ignition systems means that no contact breaker is used. Some high performance and luxury saloon cars are now appearing on the market with transistorised ignition systems, the Jaguar XJ12 being just one.

## Power for lights, horns and accessories

A glance at a car manufactured only 15 to 20 years ago will show how few electrical gadgets were "built-in" to the car's electrical system. Over the years, with increasing interest shown in greater safety, high power and auxiliary lighting for motorway driving, "in car entertainment" (radios, slot stereo and so on), the loads on the battery have been ever increasing.

How does the battery not seem to lose energy?

All the drain on the battery (up to 40 amps may be needed to power the starter motor which has to spin the

# The spark that gives life to a car, the power to see the road, clean the screen, light a cigar, play a tune . . . . and a myriad other things — a car's electrics

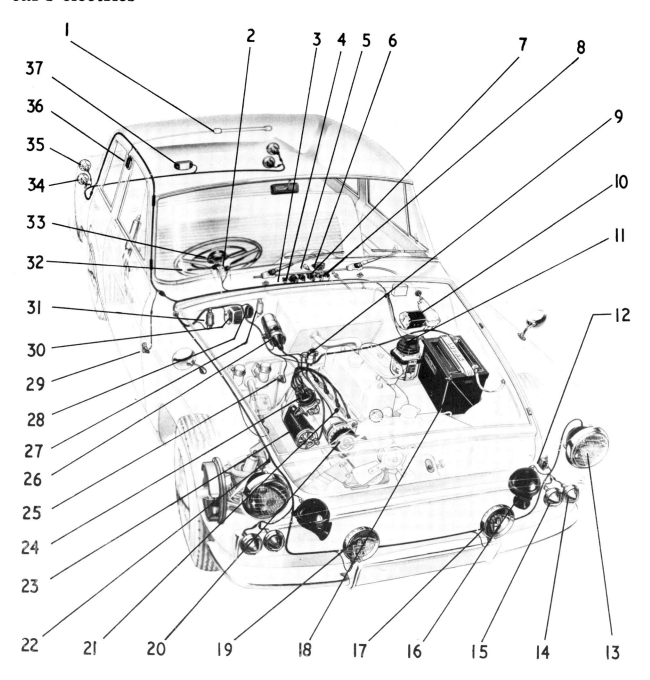

1, Interior Light; 2, Headlight Dip Switch; 3, Panel Light Switch; 4, Ignition/Start; 5, Ignition Warning Light; 6, Fuel Gauge; 7, Main Light Switch; 8, Windscreen Screen Wipers; 9, Starter Relay; 10, Wiper Motor; 11, Elec. Screen Washer; 12, Horn Relay; 13, Headlamp; 14, Side Lamp; 15, Direction Flasher; 16, Horn; 17, Fog Lamp; 18, Battery; 19, Spot Lamp; 20, Alternator (or Generator); 21, High Tension Leads and Spark Plugs; 22, Wiring Loom; 23, Starter; 24, Distributor; 25, Brake Light Switch; 26, Coil; 27, Emergency Flasher; 28, Fuse Box; 29, Courtesy Light Switch; 30, Voltage Regulator; 31, Flasher Relay; 32, Flasher Controls; 33, Horn Push; 34, Rear Light/Brake Light; 35, Rear Flasher; 36, Parking Light; 37, Rear Number Plate Light.

heavy flywheel in order to turn the engine over before she'll run under her own power) must be put back in somehow. This is the job of the generator (often called the dynamo or its modern counterpart, the alternator). The generator is driven off the car's fan belt via a belt and pulley arrangement and supplies the car's electrical power once the engine is running above a predetermined speed.

Once the engine passes what we would call "tick-over" speed, the generator is brought into play to feed a manufactured electrical re-charge to the battery.

Most family saloons in the middle to expensive price range are fitted with an instrument called an ammeter which tells the driver the charging rate being offered by the generator. Apart from replacing the energy expended by the battery in starting, the dynamo also helps to replace that taken out by all the other electrical fittings on the car.

HEADLAMPS and SIDE LIGHTS: Most headlamps are now of the "sealed beam" type and are made by a very involved and highly technical process with the special lighting filaments correctly positioned between the reflector area and the front lamp glass. Sidelamps are slowly going out of fashion as it has been recognised that a larger area of dim light is easier for oncoming motorists to see especially in foggy or snowy conditions. However sidelights are still fitted to many cars and normally find flashing direction indicators as neighbours.

DIRECTION FLASHERS are an amber colour to differentiate them from the similarly sized white sidelights and red tail lamps. They must flash within specific limits — not too fast, not too slow — to be safe and legally acceptable.

REAR LIGHTS and BRAKE LIGHTS   As soon as conditions require lights to be used, and the driver presses the switch, the two front sidelights will come on along with the two red lights denoting the rear extremities of the car. As soon as the driver places any pressure on the brake pedal, the car's brake lights are brought into operation and glow brighter than the red running lights in order to warn motorists behind of his action.

INTERIOR LIGHTS: There are various lights fitted to the interior of a modern car. They range from instrument lighting to assist the driver at night, to the courtesy light which comes on to illuminate the inside whenever the passenger's or the driver's door is opened. There are others such as the glove box compartment light, ash-tray and possibly map reading lights which may be fitted. The lighting to an automatic gearbox control lever also helps the driver to find his place in the dark.

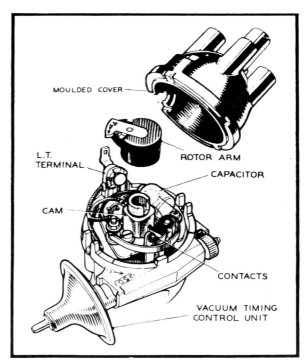

Inside the distributor — see description on page 55.

Warning lights in various colours, denoting a failure of some part of the car's system are also illuminated but these come on at any time of day or night to warn the driver of the failure, e.g. oil pressure warning light, ignition light, handbrake-on warning, and so forth.

INSTRUMENTS: Most instruments fitted to a modern car operate electrically. The only one which is usually mechanically operated is the speedometer.

WINDSCREEN WIPERS: The bad-old-days of hand-operated, then clockwork, and finally vacuum operated windscreen wipers have gone. Today an electric motor will drive the wiper blades. Some motors can be set for slow or fast operation and higher-priced cars may be fitted with a variable speed control for increased safety in drizzly conditions. Windscreen washers can also be electrically operated.

ACCESSORIES: Most motorists like to fit additional equipment to bring the car's facilities up to his own requirements. The most popular accessories include additional lights (spot lamps, fog lamps, and reversing lights), a radio or slot-stereo system, and for safety, a heated rear windscreen to keep rearward vision clear by removing mist and ice from the rear window.

Then there is a myriad of gadgets such as electrically operated radio aerials, cigar lighters, map lights, and on luxury cars even air conditioning equipment, electrically operated windows and many more.

The well equipped cockpit and interior of a Fiat 130/3200 saloon. A key to the items included appears on the next page.

Getting to know . . .

# A CAR'S INSTRUMENTS

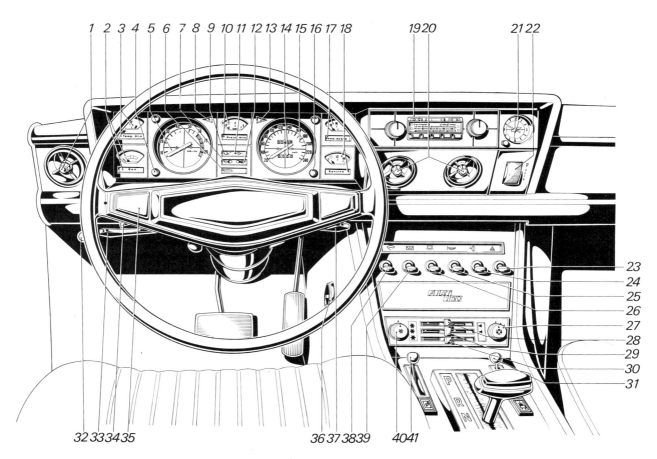

1 2 3 4 5 6 7 8 9 10 11 12 13 14 15 16 17 18    19 20    21 22

23
24
25
26
27
28
29
30
31

32 33 34 35    36 37 38 39    40 41

# What the dials tell the driver

## SPEEDOMETER

The speedometer is the only instrument that must, by law, be fitted to every car. It usually consists of a round dial fitted to the instrument panel or dashboard, and tells the driver the speed at which the car is travelling.

The dial is usually marked in units of ten miles per hour (m.p.h.) and the road speed is indicated by a pointer needle. Another type has a coloured band operated by a revolving drum and moving along a horizontal scale.

The speedometer is connected by a flexible drive cable to either a front wheel or the drive side of the gearbox.

## ODOMETER

The odometer is better known to most people as the mileage recorder and is usually incorporated in the speedometer dial. Some speedometers give two odometer readings; one showing the total mileage and the other the current journey mileage.

## FUEL GAUGE

The fuel gauge on the dashboard indicates the amount of petrol in the car's petrol tank. A float in the petrol tank which rises or falls with the fuel level is connected with the gauge. The gauge is now normally activated by an electric current which is controlled by the float.

## WATER TEMPERATURE GAUGE

This works in much the same way as the petrol gauge, but the amount of electric current passing through the gauge is controlled by a sensor unit mounted into the engine's water jacket. The hotter the water gets, the more current flows through a coil-heating bi-metal strip which moves the needle on the gauge.

A temperature gauge can show either an exact reading in degrees or C (cold), N (normal) and H (hot).

## OIL-PRESSURE GAUGE

The oil pressure gauge shows the pressure of oil in the engine's lubrication system. A flexible tube coiled inside the gauge is connected to the engine by a pipe. As oil pressure builds up, the tube tends to uncoil and in doing so, moves the needle on the dial to indicate the oil pressure.

A reading much lower than normal may indicate wear in the engine's main bearings. Erratic readings, particularly when cornering, indicate that the level of oil in the engine sump is too low. Most cars have an oil-pressure warning light instead of a gauge.

## TACHOMETER

A tachometer, often referred to as a rev (revolution) counter, is fitted usually to sports, fast touring and racing cars. Operated either electrically or mechanically, it shows the speed at which the engine crankshaft is rotating in revolutions per minute. The dial is usually marked in units of ten and the reading must be multiplied by 100 to give the r.p.m.

## AMMETER

The ammeter indicates the amount of current flowing to or from the battery and thus the rate at which the battery is being charged or discharged. On some cars, an ammeter is fitted instead of an ignition warning light.

A broken fan belt will cause the ammeter to show a discharge since the belt is not driving the dynamo and the battery is not being charged. Any defects in the dynamo or charging circuit will also show as a discharge on the ammeter.

While the car's electrical system is working normally and the battery is in a reasonable state of charge, the ammeter should show a fairly high reading for the first few minutes after the car has been started as the current used by the starter motor is replaced in the battery. The reading will then drop back to indicate a low trickle charge.

---

### KEY TO INSTRUMENTS FITTED TO A FIAT 130 SALOON (LEFT HAND DRIVE)

| | | |
|---|---|---|
| 1 Heated or fresh air outlets | 16 Trip recorder zeroing knob | 30 Conditioner through-flow air intake control |
| 2 Generator voltmeter | 17 Water thermometer with indicator | 31 Choke control |
| 3 Oil temperature | 18 Fuel gauge with reserve indicator | 32 Heated or fresh air outlets control |
| 4 Instrument lighting rheostat | 19 Radio (optional extra) | 33 High/low beams change-over switch |
| 5 Tachometer | 20 Air delivery outlets | 34 Direction indicators control |
| 6 Back window demister indicator | 21 Electronic clock | 35 Horn control |
| 7 Parking lights indicator | 22 Windshield defrost control | 36 Conditioned air outlets |
| 8 Left turn signal tell-tale | 23 Spare switch | 37 Windshield wiper and washer control |
| 9 Hand brake ON indicator | 24 Fog lamp switch (optional extra) | 38 Windshield wiper switches |
| 10 Oil pressure gauge | 25 Horn switch | 39 Back window demister switch |
| 11 Choke-ON indicator | 26 Pillar lamp switch | 40 Conditioned air temperature adjustment control (optional) |
| 12 High beams ON idicator | 27 Electrofan control | 41 Throttle control |
| 13 Right turn signal tell-tale | 28 Fresh air intake control | |
| 14 Trip recorder | 29 Hot water cock control | |
| 15 Speedometer | | |

# Getting to know . . .

# LUBRICATION AND THE CAR

**Mobil Oil Co. Ltd.,
invite us
behind the scenes**

THINK of all the beautifully smooth and polished surfaces which rub together in an engine. They all started from quite rough pieces of metal whose surfaces carried thousands of lumps and cavities. They still do — it all depends on what you call "smooth".

Take a large and very rough slab of iron. Knock off the larger lumps or high spots with a hammer and chisel. Cut down the smaller ones with a milling machine. Grind them smaller still with an emery wheel and then even smaller with jeweller's rouge and elbow grease. You'll be able to see your face in it by that time but there will still be small lumps on it — *very* small lumps — but lumps just the same.

Now cut the slab in half and start to slide one half across the other. What happens?

The minute lumps on one surface knock against those on the other — some bend, some break off. Those which break off may get in the way of undamaged ones and damage both these and themselves before they fall clear as dust — more commonly known as wear debris.

All this bending, tearing and breaking gives rise to the resistance which we know as friction or drag. And to bend, break or tear anything requires energy — the very same energy that the motorist pays precious pounds for at filling stations.

## Wear

We can polish down hard lumps or soft ones until they are microscopic, but they are still lumps, and they will steal our energy as they plough through each other. Also, if we allow little lumps of dirt to join in, the rate of wear goes up alarmingly. There is, therefore, only one way to stop them — keep them away from each other — and this is what one kind of lubrication does.

## Hydrodynamic or Full Fluid Film Lubrication

The word "hydrodynamic" means "Moving water". Think of a surf board or pair of water skis. In particular think of the type often seen being towed behind a motor boat. Skis behave very much as does a metal surface moving over oil.

If we look into why skis behave as they do, it all comes back to those objectionable little lumps we mentioned earlier, or, rather, to the nooks and crannies between them.

When the skis start to move, more water tries to get in at the front and there isn't room for it. Some of the water already there leaks out from the sides but it can't find its way through all those nooks and crannies as fast as the fresh water is forced in. To make room something has to give — it's the skis — and up comes the front ends and we now have the water in the shape of a wedge with the skis continually climbing up and trying to squash it flat at one and the same time.

Exactly the same action takes place when a metal surface moves over a film of oil and the engineer is very grateful for it as it enables him to keep an expensive component skimming closely over another one without the two actually rubbing together and doing each other harm.

But these are flat surfaces. What about curved ones such as we have in a car's main bearings? Well, we just have a curved wedge of oil . . . and it works just the same. As soon as the shaft starts to move it climbs up the wedge just as the skis did and quickly reaches a position slightly out of centre where it eventually settles down.

## Boundary Lubrication

We can best follow boundary lubrication if we consider full fluid film lubrication for a little longer.

We have our skis moving or our shaft rotating, each supported on a liquid wedge. What happens when movement stops? Clearly the skis sink or the shaft settles until it actually touches its bearing. Liquid pours away from beneath them, but, when all is over, the surfaces are still wet, or at least, damp. As a result odd particles of water or oil are left behind in the crannies and if only slight movement occurs — that is to say not enough to force fresh liquid in to form another wedge — we get the old tearing and breaking of lumps starting again. This time, however, odd bits of oil or water will occasionally get between the colliding lump and soften the blow. Nevertheless, blows will occur and give rise to a lot of friction and wear. In fact almost all wear takes place during periods of boundary lubrication and practically none when a full fluid film exists.

## Oils

Nobody is quite certain how or when crude oil collected in large lakes under certain parts of the earth's crust. It is generally thought that it was formed from

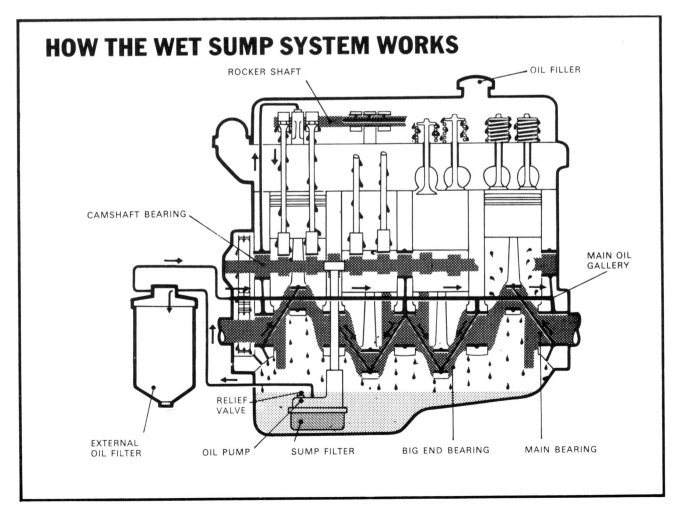

# HOW THE WET SUMP SYSTEM WORKS

ROCKER SHAFT

OIL FILLER

CAMSHAFT BEARING

MAIN OIL GALLERY

RELIEF VALVE

EXTERNAL OIL FILTER

OIL PUMP

SUMP FILTER

BIG END BEARING

MAIN BEARING

decaying marine vegetable matter and crude forms of marine animal life which were crushed at fantastic temperatures and pressures as the world cooled off thousands of centuries ago. The word petroleum comes from the Latin *petra* and *cleum* — rock oil.

## Crude Oils

Crude petroleum is generally found in liquid forms. Some are so thick as to be almost solid. These are the asphalts. Some of the other end of the scale are very thin — even gases. There is a whole range of what may be termed "in betweens", many of which may be found together in any one deposit. In the purified state, all are compounds of carbon and hydrogen. They may be tainted with other elements, which must be removed and reduced before they can be used safely in machinery.

There are thousands of different ways in which carbon and hydrogen can combine, but all products resulting from such combinations are known as hydrocarbons.

## Refining

The job of the oil refinery is to separate the thousands of different hydrocarbons that may be in one particular crude oil into groups of fairly similar ones. Because there are so many different hydrocarbons it is hardly possible to single out odd ones, and anyway it is very hard to tell the difference between some of them.

As to *how* to do it, the oil refinery takes advantage of the fact that different groups boil at different temperatures. Engine oil and petrol are both hydrocarbons, so for the sake of argument let's mix them up and then try to separate them again. We put them in a pot and heat them up but take the precaution of removing any air which would help them to burn. When we reach about 100 deg. F., the petrol will start to boil. All we do is to let it — and collect the "steam" or vapour. When we cool the vapour, we get liquid petrol again — free from the oil which never got to the boil.

For goodness sake do not try this at home! Highly controlled laboratory conditions are necessary to prevent an explosion.

This is how it is done in practice, except that a refinery uses a very tall pot called a fractionating column and doesn't just start with only two hydrocarbons. The higher we go up the column, the cooler it gets, so that different vapours start to turn back into liquids at different levels.

Trays are provided to collect the various liquids, in groups remember, and such groups may then have to be sent through other processes, later to be broken down into further groups, or modified to improve their usefulness.

The base oils and petrol stocks are subsequently purified, blended compounded and treated with additives to give finished products each suitable for a specific purpose.

Besides oil and fuels, an enormous number of other products can be extracted from a crude oil. These products may be further processed into such varied commodities as face cream, gramophone records and weed killer.

## Specifications

Because of the number of different ingredients in any one oil it is impossible to specify its *precise* quality or composition. There is no test or set of tests which can measure the "oilness" of an oil and it has been found by long experience that motor oils for instance can only be judged usefully to their performance on the road in every type of machine they will be expected to use in. Oil companies employ several types of testing machines but mainly they use real engines and real back axles because at times one machine would fail an oil which passed with flying colours on another. Testing machines have a few advantages, but the only true testing machines are the engine, gearbox and back axle of a car.

## Viscosity

Viscosity measures the stiffness — NOT the oiliness — of an oil. Viscosity is, however, one of the most important qualities of an oil as it decides load carrying ability and power loss; in other words — the viscosity decides the fluid-film-forming ability. The higher the viscosity the greater load an oil can carry, but high viscosity obviously makes for stiffer movement and hence affects a motorist's miles per gallon reading. If too viscous, the oil could be very difficult to pump or pour especially in winter time. Viscosity also decides the rate of possible leakage and ease of starting.

Viscosity used to be measured by the time, in seconds, that it took for a certain amount of oil to flow through a hole in the bottom of a pot. It was a very special hole of accurate dimensions and often made of agate so that it wouldn't get worn or damaged. Nowadays, more complicated apparatus is used but all the instruments are called "viscometers".

Obviously the same oil can run through that hole quicker if it is hot and thin rather than if cooler and thicker. Unless the temperature is specified therefore, a viscosity reading means nothing.

The big thing for car engines is to make an oil which doesn't get too thick in winter or too thin in summer and to get it to stay that way.

An RAC Observer ensures that a Mobil engineer keeps to his test schedule when carrying out observations of oil performance in a Ford Escort Mexico.

## Lubricity or Oiliness

Important though viscosity is, it is not the only thing which makes an oil. Its viscosity will largely determine its ability to form a wedge or full fluid film but treacle or hot glue could have the same viscosity and produce a similar film!

What decides their oiliness, or their ability to provide boundary lubrication, seems to depend partly on how they attach themselves to a surface and on how their molecular structure is arranged. It is also believed to be connected with their relative moduli or rigidity and of tension. It is all very involved and the backroom boys have not yet quite sorted it all out! You can, however, take it that oiliness is not necessarily related to viscosity but whatever the theory, the finest practice is to judge the results.

## Stability

The dictionary calls this "steadfastness" or "constancy". Chemically speaking, stability means "not easily decomposed, rotted, rusted or turned into something else".

Now, iron isn't chemically stable. When moist air gets at it, the oxygen in the air attacks the iron — oxidises it

as we say — to form rust. Oils oxidise too. They don't form rust, though, but carbon and water. Leave a saucer of oil to itself (and the air) for a century or two and a thin crust will form on the top. If you keep it hot it will oxidise much more quickly. If you keep it very hot it will burst into flames. Burning is only very rapid oxidation — like a vicious circle of heat producing oxidation — producing heat — producing oxidation — and so on.

Obviously then, as an oil has to live in places such as a car's cylinder bores, where there is a great deal of heat, it must have as low a rate of oxidation as possible. As all oils burn, and oxidation is only slow burning the difficulty cannot completely be overcome, but careful choice of desirable crudes with correct refining will remove most of the easily-attacked hydrocarbons and leave an oil of high stability.

The rate of oxidation of an oil can also be reduced by adding compounds known as oxidation inhibitors or antioxidants. These may sound very highfalutin' but they are only special chemicals which oxygen likes better than oil. Such inhibitors themselves become oxidised in time, however, and then deterioration of the oil carries on as before.

## Detergency

Even in highly refined oils having oxidation inhibitors, deposits of sludge, lacquer and carbon gradually accumulate; a lot comes from burnt petrol. If this accumulation is not checked blockage of oilways and filters may result. In any case, sludge and carbon will form in piston ring grooves, eventually causing the rings to stick.

It is, however, possible to treat oils, or rather to treat their impurities as they form so that they cannot collect in large lumps. The materials which do this are known as dispersive detergents. If large lumps have already formed, no detergent will shift them — whatever the old diehards may tell you.

The specks of impurity are extremely small and will pass easily through a normal filter. Filters used with detergent oils always remain surprisingly clean — the oil itself of course becomes darkened quite rapidly.

## Other Properties

Besides viscosity, stability, lubricity and detergency, other qualities of oils, such as foaming or corrosive tendencies have to be taken into account. Refinery-blended addition agents are used, with discretion, when it is desired to emphasise any particular property of an oil in its refined but otherwise untreated state. That is to say that, to a certain extent, we can add chemicals to oils to make them more "oily", more detergent, or to alter other characteristics for special purposes such as hypoid gears of large diesel engines.

## Greases

Greases are not just still oils or fats. They are generally made from ordinary lubricating oils held together in a plastic state by a soap — a soap because there are many different soaps.

Soaps are usually made from fatty oils (from animal or vegetable matter) by chemical reaction with an alkali. An alkali is normally formed when some of the rarer kinds of metal are hydrated or treated with water.

Calcium and sodium are two such metals. They are as soft as cheese and rush away completely before your very eyes if you even breathe on them. You will know the alkalis they form as quicklime and caustic soda.

Other metals used to form grease soaps include lithium, aluminium and lead, and the greases made from lithium are miles ahead of the others in every way. Nowadays, there are different ways of making even better greases still.

Most oil companies sponsor rally drivers. Their findings and the engine's performance are "in situ" tests under extremes of motoring conditions.

## Desirable Properties of a Grease

The main, and perhaps obvious, purpose of a grease is to provide a lubricant which will stay put and not leak or wash away. While being stiff enough to stay put it must not be so stiff as to cause drag and, of course, it must be soft enough to be pumped and to pass through the lubrication nipples to the working surfaces.

In such components as a car's wheel hubs, a grease must be able to stand the high temperatures often developed by the brakes and as the grease is, of course, composed of soap and lubricating oil, it is the melting point of the soap which decides this ability.

A grease used for ball or roller-bearing lubrication must not soften or stiffen unduly in use. If it becomes too soft it can drain away from the critical parts of the bearing.

Greases must not be corrosive and, if possible, they should not be affected by water.

## The search for "new" oils

THE CAR MAKERS can only produce an inaminate lump of metalurgical design — without a power source (petrol, electricity, steam etc) a car cannot function. Without oil to lubricate working parts it cannot keep running.

Every oil company is constantly on the search for better oil products to cope with the ever-increasing demand by private and commerical road users. They are battling against difficult odds — the ever-declining availability of natural crude oils which are used and after various degrees of refinement, the addition of various "additives", give us the lubricants the motorist buys from the garage shelf.

As we have said, engine lubricants, whether they are oils or greases, have one common primary role — they have to interpose themselves between metal surfaces so that these can move relative to each other without actually touching. The lubricants become in effect millions of microscopic ball bearings, rolling instead of rubbing.

This would not be too onerous a task for any reasonably stable liquid if engines always ran at constant moderate speeds under constant loads and under temperate ambient conditions. In practice, speeds, bearing loads and operating temperatures vary enormously even under ordinary motoring conditions. Seasonal changes in ambient temperatures can create quite artificial variations in the state of the lubricant itself.

As with other large industries, oil companies use computers to control plant processes accurately so controlling quality to the last degree.

"... Our hopes for years to come." The world was stunned to find itself without plentiful oil supplies. It is with thanks that Britain can once again turn to the sea in a time of trouble. This is *Transocean* No. 1, a mobile self-elevating offshore drilling platform which has been operating off the Leman Bank in the North Sea. New distillation processes could even produce better fuels — who knows. Those deeply concerned with Europe's economics just wait, and hope.

Perhaps the most extreme example of this demand for consistency in lubricant performance under wide variations of temperature was the case of Concorde. Its engines had to meet extremes of 200 deg. C (twice the boiling point of water) in the engines while the air temperature was as low as —40 deg. C. This seems an impossible target, but it has been met by a synthetic hydrocarbon product.

No car has to face such extreme demands as this, but the requirements of modern car engines can be quite tough from the lubricant standpoint. Year by year engine power output per cc goes up and with it the bearing loads and operating temperatures go up as well. The engine oil has another important function besides sheer lubrication; it has to act as a coolent. The oil circulates around the hot bearings, the very hot valve gear and the even hotter pistons and rings, then returns *via* the filter to the sump where it has a short time to cool off before going round again.

On the face of it a large sump capacity would seem to be the answer. But, apart from the important space and weight considerations involved, over-cooling could be a serious disadvantage in winter conditions. The oil would be too thick to circulate freely; pressures would be high but bearings could be starved.

Excellent as current automotive lubrication oils are, they sometimes fail to reach the standards required by cars of the GT classification and those which are subjected to exceptional stress levels. Caravaners, for example are nowadays advised to fit additional oil coolers if they propose to tow in mountainous districts.

Continuous development goes on by oil manufacturers, and it was to resolve these problems, as well as the requirements of competition rally drivers, that SHC (Synthesised Hydro Carbon) oil was developed by Mobil.

A good engine oil has to meet the demand of punishing motoring — in Rally service, for high-speed motorway driving, where trailer towing imposes heavy loads, or where the car engines suffer from falling oil pressure which may bring in the red light at high temperatures and low engine speeds.

Such conditions can impose a severe challenge for an oil. A recently published survey by the Co-ordinating European Council of the Motor and Petroleum Industry showed that many car builders are experiencing very high sump temperatures. Many are in the 150 deg. C region. These temperatures are often reached under steady high speed driving conditions in summer for prolonged periods. The CEC Group also asked Europe's car makers what their design needs for the future were. Future sump temperatures were forecast to rise by 10 to 15 deg. C over the next five years. A significant number of builders wanted the oil industry to design for 160 deg. C maximum in the future.

THE PETROL or "motor spirit" that we pump, gallon after gallon, into our cars is a derivitive of that thick, gooey substance known as crude oil. The major oil producing countries, mainly the Arab states, sell us their crude oil which we bring by means of huge ocean-going tankers to oil refineries like those at Coryton in Essex, at Milford Haven in Pembrokeshire, and Fawley in Hampshire.

At the 23 refineries in the United Kingdom, distillation is carried out in tall, massive columns known as fractionising towers. Many other bi-products are also drawn off as the crude oil is heated to vaporise its various constituants. But the petrol drawn off after vaporisation in the fractionising towers has to be further processed and refined to make it suitable for use in our cars.

# Getting to know . . .

# PETROL

During its refinement, the petrol has such undesirable properties as gum-forming elements, corrosive mixtures, and the like removed until eventually it can be brought up to the required British Standard for which it will receive a star rating. It will be blended and treated with additives which will improve various desirable properties such as its resistance to detonation (the unacceptably rapid burning of the petrol/air mixture in a combustion chamber which gives rise to serious piston damage and can be recognised by listening for a mettalic "pinging" when the engine is running).

## Which Star Grade?

At one time, one pump gave one petrol grade but modern self-service stations normally have a row of perhaps four pumps which will be known as "blender pumps". These can be set to deliver various blends to suit the star rating required.

The British Standards Institution ratings mean that two stars are used by garages to indicate the lowest octane number — 90. Three stars are given to grades with a minimum octane value of 94 and maximum of 96. Four star petrol, which is by far the most widely used according to the statistics, covers octane values between 97 and 99. Five stars are awarded only to fuel of 100 octane.

Every car manufacturer states the recommended petrol grade for each of the models he makes and an owner will gain nothing (except a hole in his pocket) by filling up with four star petrol if the engine is designed to run on two star. The choice of petrol grade depends to a large extent on the compression ratio of the engine. A high compression engine will normally need a higher octane petrol than a lower compression one.

## Petrol Economy

During the mini-crisis in November 1973 the Royal Automobile Club advised motorists that the best way to get more miles to the gallon was by using the accelerator carefully. Roaring away from traffic lights with your foot on the floorboard may be exciting but if you had a "money-eater" meter fitted to your car you'd soon give the accelerator a light touch and build up engine revs steadily.

Many other things can affect a car's petrol economy from ensuring that the ignition system is in good shape, to having the carburettor accurately set by an experienced mechanic, and even to checking that the handbrake is completely off and tyres are at the correct pressure.

It has been intimated that petrol could cost as much as a pound a gallon within a few years. Every driver would then take very earnest measures to ensure that his car was handled with fuel economy always in mind!

Just as we take cars so much for granted, so do we assume that we can just roll into any garage and fill up with as much petrol as we need. It needed that mini-crisis in '73 to bring home to every motorist that without petrol, the car is obsolete — at least until the all-electric car is a viable proposition. Petrol rationing, a threat with which we shall be living for many years as oil production comes hard pressed to meet demand, will make us all petrol-misers every time we turn an ignition key!

## Oil from beneath the sea

Though we used something over 3½ million tons of petrol last year, most of which was imported in the form of crude oil which our refineries processed, it is important not to forget the possibilities that before 1980 we could be receiving our first barrels of oil from the North Sea oil wells. There have been several discoveries, some small, some significantly large, not only in our own waters but off Norway and the Netherlands.

Problems of delivery to the mainland will have to be solved once the feasibility of drilling the various continental shelves is overcome. But where there's a will . . . there'll be a well.

A Ford Capri on the Mobil Economy Run

EVERY MOTORIST has to take his car to a garage for service or repair at some time or another. Choosing the right garage is an important part of motoring, and learning how to use it to the best advantage is a lesson which every motorist should learn. In this way many of the disputes and much of the bad temper, waste of time and loss of money which plagues so many motorists, could be avoided.

It is only right to expect prompt attention and good workmanship at a reasonable price; but all garages are not equally suited to deal with your make of car. The complexity of the modern vehicle makes it essential for major repairs to be carried out at garages which have the specialised tools and equipment for the job and mechanics trained to use them. A garage which is the manufacturer's authorised franchise-holder is, therefore, obviously the best one to choose.

The range in garages varies considerably, from the filling-station type selling petrol, oil and a few accessories, to the "super" garage which deals with insurance, car hire, new and used car sales and major body and mechanical repairs. It is unreasonable to expect the same extent of service from both types of garage.

But the motorist who knows what he wants can choose accordingly. To find a garage of his choice he can consult the manufacturer, one of the motoring organisations, or follow the recommendations of a friend. As in other spheres of life, one method of ensuring reliable service is to become a regular. A motorist who goes to a garage for petrol, spares and routine work becomes a valued customer and is more likely to get extra assistance when in difficulties.

Having found an apparently suitable garage, the motorist obviously expects to get the best out of it. But he must be prepared to play his part; for example, when taking a car to a garage to be repaired he should always give the symptoms to the receptionist and not what he believes to be wrong. If he tells the garage to do a particular repair or service they may just go and do that, and a motorist has no comeback if this fails to correct the fault. The best method is to rely on the experience of the garage mechanic to diagnose the trouble.

# Getting to know . . .

# THE
# GARAGE

Manufacturers usually recommend servicing at intervals of 3,000 or 6,000 miles, or, if this comes sooner, every three months; so it will not be long before the motorist has to call on a garage. The items of work necessary at each service have been compiled from many years' experience and include additional checks to make sure that a car complies with the law. With regular servicing, faults which might otherwise develop into serious and dangerous defects can usually be detected before they go too far. With the drill for servicing laid down so exactly, if you require any additional work done to the car you give details when booking a service.

During the servicing, if other faults come to light, fix a convenient date for repairs to be carried out. Prior notice enables garages to make sure that parts will be available. Other ways of recognising the need for pending repairs include a general falling off in efficiency or a partial failure causing a minor breakdown.

Repairs of this kind, made necessary by normal wear, include tuning the engine, fitting new suspension elements, relining brakes, overhauling clutch and fitting new tyres. Ideally, dents and body damage should be dealt with by garages with their own panel-beating facilities, otherwise garages usually send work of this type to a specialist firm.

The factor which is so often a bone of contention between motorists and garage is the cost of the job. Frankly, most motorists' idea of repair costs are generally wide of the mark. The garage charge for repair work is made up of two elements; retail cost of any parts supplied, and the cost of labour charged at an hourly rate. The labour charges vary from one part of the country to another, but usually there is little or no difference between franchise and non-franchise garages in the same area.

The simple answer, of course, is *always* ask for it in writing. There are occasions, however, when it may not be possible for the garage to give a reliable estimate without first dismantling parts and investigating the cause of the trouble. In this case a motorist should ask for an estimate of the cost of the exploratory work, and also what the repair itself is likely to cost.

If he feels that the estimate of the cost of repair is too high, and he takes his car to a second garage, he should be prepared to pay the first one a fair charge for the investigation work. If the costs seems too high you can always seek advice from a third party, such as the AA.

When a garage starts work on the car, the mechanics sometimes find that additional work is necessary. A good garage will not go ahead without permission, but to be on the safe side always set a cash limit to meet this contingency, and give the garage a telephone number where you can be reached during working hours if this sum is likely to be exceeded.

Apart from the cost, a motorist naturally wants to know how long the repair will take. If the car is needed at

A medium-size garage in Hawkhurst, Kent. The services and layout of such a garage appear on the next two pages.

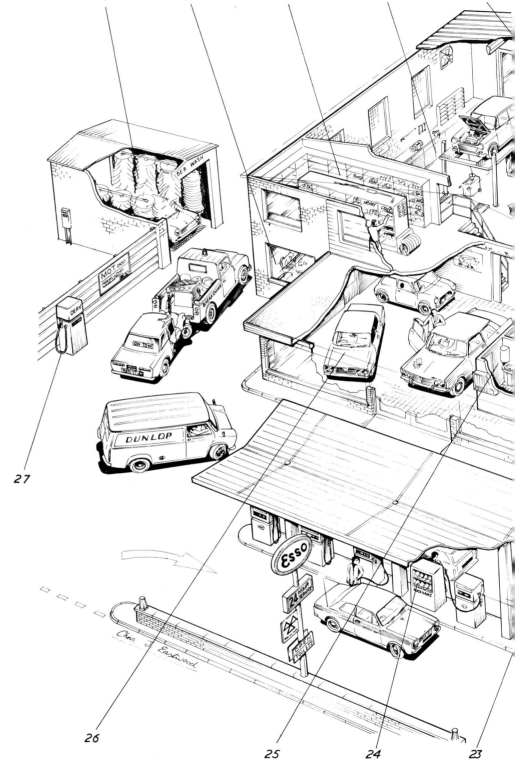

1 Car Wash
2 Offices
3 Stores — engine components etc.
4 Electrically-operated ramp and lubrication bay
5 Hydraulic lubrication equipment
6 General service bay
7 Sun Tuner
8 Tyre changing machine
9 Wheel balancing machine
10 Compressor shed (used for paint spraying equipment, etc.)
11 Gas Welding equipment
12 Body shop (for damaged cars)
13 Engine hoist
14 Air line
15 Extractor fan (paint fumes)
16 Paint shop (re-spray)
17 Second-hand cars for sale
18 Motorists Shop (maps, wiper blades, tools, bulbs, polishes, etc. etc.)
19 Fuel tank vents
20 Underground petrol tank
21 Tank filler and dip stick
22 Self-service pay and adding machines. Reception Area
23 Self-service pumps
24 Oils, anti-freeze, distilled water etc.
25 Toilets
26 New Car showroom
27 Diesel pump
28 Paraffin vending machine

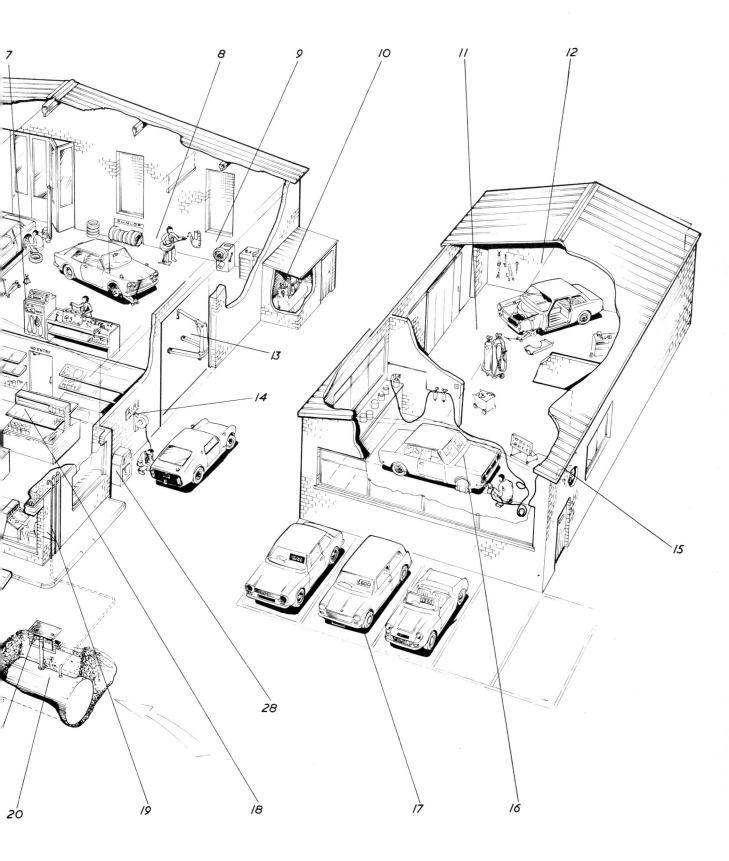

7       8       9      10      11      12

13

14

15

28

20      19      18      17      16

Just part of a garage's hardware — trolley, bottle, and scissor jacks, hydraulic cranes, axle stands, portable analysers.

Engine analysers are playing an increasing roll in the efficient running of even smaller garages. They can tell a trained operative in seconds what would otherwise take hours to check.

A tyre changer is almost essential equipment for a workshop. A wheel balancing machine would also, probably, be found nearby.

Below: Wheel alignment apparatus can quickly check a wheel's camber, amount of "toe in" or "toe out", and castor angle.

a particular time on a particular day it is best to ensure the garage can do the job. It is always best, where possible to allow extra time, because any number of unforeseen circumstances may arise to delay the garage — such as lack of special parts, or an industrial dispute. A motorist has little redress if his car is not ready at the time promised, even though delay causes inconvenience or financial loss. In practice all he can do is to take his custom elsewhere in future.

Disputes with garages are far too common. The AA alone deals with more than 70,000 a year. If a motorist does become involved it is advisable to follow the correct procedure.

First, the motorist should take up the complaint with the garage manager. There is nothing to be gained by bringing in a third party until your case is put directly to the people involved. If the complaint is about the repair itself, and a fair one, there is a good chance that the garage will look into it.

If the complaint fails to produce a satisfactory result then bring in a third party. If the garage, for instance, has an AA spanner or breakdown grading it will have agreed to co-operate with the Association in attempting to resolve amicably any dispute with an AA member. In such cases the AA's own team of expert engineers will frequently succeed in sorting out the problem.

Dispute with garages which do not belong to the scheme may not be so easy to settle.

The motorist who does not belong to a motoring organisation can still enlist help in a dispute with a garage.

One channel is the trade itself. If the garage is a franchise-holder, the motorist can complain to the manufacturer, who may be prepared to look into the case.

If the garage belongs to the Motor Agents' Association, which is a trade body, the motorist can refer the case to the MAA Investigation and Advisory Service at 201 Great Portland Street, London W.1. A similar scheme is operated in Scotland by the Scottish Motor Trade Association at 3 Palmerston Place, Edinburgh, EH12 5AQ.

In any dispute with a garage, the ultimate recourse is to legal action. In some instances a letter from the motorist's solicitor may persuade a garage to compromise. In others it may be necessary to go through the expensive and time-consuming business of going to court.

Solicitors usually advise against this unless the claim is for a large sum of money. Indeed it has been calculated that most people going to court with a claim for less than £30 actually end up out of pocket — even if they win their case and have costs awarded in their favour.

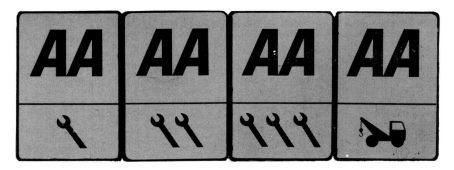

## SPANNER SPOTTING . . .

ONE SPANNER represents the small town, suburban and rural garage with adequate facilities for customers and at least half its adult staff fully trained. It will be able to adjust and replace all major mechanical components for a particular range of vehicles, and will have special tools, parts and accessories.

Apart from routine servicing, these are the jobs you can expect a one-spanner garage to undertake: valve re-grind, decarb or complete replacement of engine; replacement of clutch, manual gearbox, wheel bearings, drive shaft, differential and final drive unit; minor adjustments to automatic gearbox; overhaul of brakes; adjustments to wheels and steering; replacement of electrical units; adjustment of headlights.

TWO SPANNERS will go to the medium-sized garage with has at least two-thirds of its staff formally trained and appropriately qualified. It will have a comfortable customer reception area, and will be able to carry out all routine service and repair tasks as well as specialised tuning and brake testing. The spare parts store will include reconditioned components for the dealerships held.

It should be able to tackle such additional jobs as complete strip-down and overhaul of engine, manual gearbox and final drive unit; adjustment of automatic transmission; replacement of brake system components; overhaul, checking, re-assembly and test of suspension, steering gear and most electrical components. This garage will also straighten, replace or repaint most body panels.

THREE SPANNERS will be awarded only to garages with the most up-to-date facilities, able to cover inspection, servicing, diagnosis and repair with the minimum need for advance booking. Almost all the adult staff will be appropriately qualified, and the specialised equipment available will be able to detect obscure electrical and mechanical faults. They will be competent to produce the highest standard of body repair and painting.

Specialist tasks include: full electronic engine diagnosis; brake roller testing; wheel and chassis alignment testing; full strip, overhaul and testing of automatic gearbox; all kinds of body repairs and repainting work.

BREAKDOWN garages will offer reliable mechanical and electrical first-aid, at least until midnight, and will carry a wide range of essential spares for most makes of car. They should have good communications with AA emergency services, and have a telephone manned during operating hours. Because motorists sometimes have to wait while their cars are being attended to, the garages should have adequate waiting room and toilet facilities, preferably with vending machines and public telephones. The breakdown garage must be able to: recover damaged or broken-down cars; replace fan belts, hoses, bulbs, engine gaskets, exhaust systems, ignition components, dynamos, starters, fuel pumps and tyres or tubes; recharge batteries.

---

EVERY CAR, once it has been used for more than three years, must be given the first of what will become yearly tests for roadworthiness. These are known by most drivers as M.O.T. tests because they were originally controlled by the Ministry of Transport, now called the Department of the Environment.

The test is carried out at a garage approved by the Department of the Environment and displaying a special sign. There are about 20,000 garages in Britain authorised to carry out M.O.T. tests, and more than 12 million vehicles are tested each year.

The car will be thoroughly examined to see that its brakes, lights, steering, tyres and seat belt anchorages comply with the legal requirements. If they do, a certificate is issued which covers the car for one year.

If any one of the components fails, the owner of the car is issued with a notification of refusal; it is then illegal for him to use the car except to drive home.

If a car fails the test, the owner can appeal to the Department of the Environment within 14 days. The car will then be re-tested.

An examiner can refuse to test a car submitted for examination if it is excessively dirty, has insufficient petrol, has an insecure load such as a roof rack with badly stowed luggage on it, or if the car's registration book is not available.

The examiner will pay particular attention to the following;
STEERING Steering linkages and mountings must be free of damage and wear; there must be no corrosion which could weaken the steering gear. There must be no excessive play in the steering mechanism.
SUSPENSION All suspension points, connections and linkages must be free of undue play or looseness and must not be excessively worn or damaged. All retaining bolts must be secure and there should be no corrosion capable of weakening the system.
BRAKES All brake linkages, connecting rods, cables and hoses must be free of damage, hydraulic leaks and wear. The handbrake must be at least 25 per cent efficient, the footbrake 50 per cent.

# Getting to know . . .

# THE M.O.T. TEST

TYRES The tread of all four tyres fitted to the car must be at least 1mm deep and the regulations concerning the mixing of tyres observed. The tyres must also be free of any cuts or bulges, particularly to the sidewalls.

LIGHTS The lights must be in working order, and the headlamps must be correctly aligned so as not to dazzle other road users. Brake lights and indicators are not subject to the test, however.

SEAT BELTS If the car is required to have seat belts fitted, they must be correctly and securely fitted.

When the examiner has completed his mechanical inspection, he may test the car either on the road or on a rolling road machine. Usually he will take it out on the road for a short run, provided he is satisfied that the car is safe enough to drive. If he cannot test drive the car, it will fail.

**The requirements of the car roadworthiness test are as follows:—**

The mechanical parts of the braking and steering systems should be effective; and the suspension system should not be faulty in any way that could adversely affect brakes or steering; the lights should be in working order and visible from 200 yards; the law requires that cars registered after December 31, 1964, should be fitted with seat belts; the tyres must comply with the regulations on tread, inflation, damage and mixing of cross-ply and radial ply. The chassis and bodywork should not be corroded or damaged to any extent which would either affect the working of the steering or braking systems or possibly cause some injury to other road users.

THE CAR ENTHUSIAST'S LANGUAGE CAN BE CONFUSING
IF NOT MISINTERPRETED. OF THE MANY TERMS YOU
WILL HEAR THE FOLLOWING HAVE BEEN CHOSEN AS
THOSE WHICH WILL HELP IN READING "Getting to Know Cars
and Motoring" AS WELL AS READING MAGAZINES AND
UNDERSTANDING ENTHUSIASTS...

# CAR TALK

**ACCELERATOR:** Normally applies to the accelerator or throttle pedal which controls the engine's speed.

**ACCUMULATOR:** A battery which can be re-charged (i.e. is not thrown away after it loses its power) can be called an accumulator.

**ACKERMAN STEERING:** The principle whereby, when steering a car in a circle or round a bend, the inner wheel takes up a greater angle than the outer wheel.

**ADDITIVES:** Chemicals that can be put in petrol and oil to increase one or several properties which might improve performance.

**ADVANCING A SPARK:** The high voltage spark in the cylinder should occur just before the piston reaches its top dead centre (t.d.c.) position. Most modern car engines feature advanced spark timing.

**AERODYNAMICALLY STYLED:** A car body which presents as little resistance to the air and hence as little drag as possible. Testing for aerodynamics is normally carried out in a wind tunnel.

**AIR-COOLED ENGINE:** No water at all is used for cooling — instead air is fanned over the engine parts which heat up.

**AIR FILTER:** Equipment fitted to filter harmful dust particles from the air before it is led to the carburettor.

**AIR HORNS:** Warning horns operated by compressed air, normally more striking than other types.

**ALIGNMENT:** The "lining up" of objects in relation to each other. Often refers to the setting up of front wheels of the car.

**ALTERNATING CURRENT:** Electric current which flows first one way, then the next. Often abreviated to a.c.

**ALTERNATOR:** A modern generator which is engine-driven and produces an Alternating Current to recharge the battery. (Unlike a dynamo which produces Direct Current).

**AMMETER:** An instrument on the dashboard which tells the driver how much charge the battery is receiving. Or how much drain electrical components are taking from the battery.

**AMPERE (or AMP):** A unit of electrical current.

**AMPERE HOUR RATING:** Given to batteries to indicate the life expectancy of a charge. e.g.: a 40 amp/hour battery will last 40 hours at 1 amp drain, 20 hours at 2 amp drain etc.

**ANTIFREEZE:** A chemical solution (containing Ethylene Glycol) added to radiator water to prevent freezing during winter months.

**ANTI-ROLL BAR:** A strong steel bar running across the front and/or rear of the car's chassis to give stiffness to the car on bends.

**AQUAPLANING:** When a tyre's tread does not clear away road water and this builds up under the tyre until it eventually rides on water; the driver finds steering and braking difficult.

**ATOMISATION:** Breaking liquids down into very fine particles — e.g. the carburettor atomises petrol which can then be mixed with air for delivery as a fine mist to combustion chambers.

**AUTOMATIC (TRANSMISSION):** A gearbox which takes all the work of gear changing on itself with the driver having to choose the "drive" position after starting, and reverse when required.

**AXLE:** A metal shaft carrying the car's wheels. Suspension parts are often bolted to the axle and then to the car body.

**AXLE RATIO:** The relation between the revolutions each minute of the propeller shaft and the actual r.p.m. of the wheels being driven. The difference is accounted for by reduction through the final drive gearing.

**BACKFIRE:** An explosion in the exhaust system like a pistol crack.

**BALL JOINT:** A common type of joint which can couple two metal or plastic components together allowing each to move freely in any direction.

**BARRELS:** Separate cylinders are described as barrels though most commonly in air-cooled engines.

**BATTERY:** A convenient form of storing electricty, necessary for starting a car, and for running electrical equipment.

**BEARING:** A means of supporting a rotating shaft (or a moving part) in order to minimise friction and wear.

**BENCH SEAT:** A seat at the front of the car which runs full width. Not as popular now as individual front seats for driver and passenger.

**BEVEL GEARS:** A means of transmitting energy and motion through 90 degrees (or other angles) e.g. from one shaft to another.

**BIG END:** The connecting rod attached to the crankpin of the crankshaft has a large end (the Big End) and a smaller end (naturally called the Small End).

**BONNET:** Part of a car's bodywork which normally hinges to give access to engine.

**BOOT:** Part of car where luggage and tools can be kept.

**BORE:** Normally refers to the diameter of cylinder.

**BOTTOM DEAD CENTRE:** (b.d.c.) The lowest point the piston reaches in the cylinder.

**BRAKE:** The general term used for method and part which slows and stops rotation of the car's wheels using friction and absorbing energy. There are drum brakes, disc brakes, and the mechanical handbrake mechanism.

**BRAKE HORSEPOWER:** The term used (b.h.p.) to indicate output of power.

**BUCKET SEAT:** Commonly used to describe individual front seats. Bucket seats are normally associated with sports cars and are designed to sit "in" rather than on to give good support when cornering.

**BUMPERS:** Normally a front and rear buffer to absorb minor knocks but now more decorative than useful. Future legislation, influenced by the USA, might mean that bumpers have to be larger and able to absorb 5 mph collisions without damage.

**BUTTERFLY:** A type of valve like a metal disc — mounted in the carburettor and controlled by the throttle.

**CAMBER ANGLE:** Road wheels are often cambered to present an angle from the vertical. If wheels are closer together at the top (negative camber) the car is more likely to be stable when cornering. Also applies to road surface sloping to sides for drainage or to assist motorist when cornering.

**CAM:** An irregularly shaped piece of metal which rotates giving a lifting motion to a lever or connecting rod. e.g. as attached to the engine's camshaft.

**CARBURETTOR:** The item which mixes petrol and air in the correct proportions for feeding to the combusion chambers.

**CARCASS:** The body of a tyre, sometimes called the tyre casing.

**CHASSIS:** A framework on which a car's body is built.

**CENTRIFUGAL FORCE:** The forcing of a body outward from its curved path e.g. the force you feel when going round a roundabout (making you slide to the left of the car).

**CHOKE:** A method of making petrol to air mixture richer by increasing fuel or decreasing air portion to assist cold starting of engine.

**CLUTCH:** A foot-operated mechanism which engages and disengages the engine from the transmission.

**TO COAST:** Car's motion under own momentum — no engine power being used. Bad practice.

**COIL:** Part of the ignition system which converts the low battery current to a high one for delivery by the distributor to the spark plugs.

**COMBUSTION:** The burning of the petrol and air mixture.

**COMPRESSION:** Increasing a gas pressure by reducing volume. Diesel engines are "compression-ignition" engines using hot, compressed air to ignite injected fuel.

**CONSTANT VELOCITY JOINTS:** Fitted to front wheel drive cars to prevent judder to the steering from the driving wheels.

**CONVERTIBLE:** Car fitted with a folding hood over the driver and passenger area.

**COUPE:** A sleeker-looking saloon car top often shorter than normal.

**CRANKCASE:** An iron or aluminium casting housing the crankshaft.

**CRANKSHAFT:** Main rotating engine part which converts up-and-down piston motion to rotary motion.

**CYLINDER BLOCK:** Casing housing the engine cylinders.

**DAMPER:** Softens car body's movement — commonly called shock absorber.

**DASH (DASHBOARD):** Panel in front of driver containing instruments etc.

**DECOKE (or Decarbonise):** to remove carbon deposits from piston crown, cylinder walls and combustion chamber to bring back performance.

**De DION:** Suspension type for rear-wheels.

**DEFROSTER/DEMISTER:** Heater switch which directs warm air on to wind-screen to clear frost and mist.

**DIFFERENTIAL:** A system of gears between the driven road wheels, which allows outer wheel to rotate faster than inner wheel when turning.

**DIP STICK:** Rod inserted into sump to show whether oil is adequate or low.

**DIP SWITCH:** Switch which controls lights from full ahead position (main beam) to a lower angle to prevent glare to oncoming drivers.

**DISC BRAKES:** System whereby a caliper operated by the footbrake pinches friction pads onto revolving metal disc which rotates with the wheel.

**DISTILLED WATER:** Water with no impurities used for topping up battery's cells of electrolyte.

**DISTRIBUTOR:** Unit which delivers high voltage spark to sparking plug. Is usually driven by the camshaft.

**DROPHEAD (COUPE):** americanism for convertible-type car.

**DUAL-CONTROLS:** Most often used when training learner motorists — driver's controls are repeated on passenger side. (e.g. brake, clutch and possibly throttle.)

**DUST CAP:** Screw on cover to tyre's air inlet valve.

**DYNAMO:** Converts mechanical energy from engine fan into electrical power to recharge battery. Now more often termed GENERATOR or ALTERNATOR.

**EARTH:** Normally connection from battery or other electrical component to body metalwork to complete the electrical return circuit.

**ELECTRODE:** Conductor for feeding of electricity in car's battery. Also the central portion of a sparking plug.

**ELECTROLYTE:** Battery solution in which electrodes are immersed — a solution of sulphuric acid and distilled water.

**ELECTRONIC IGNITION:** Method of producing up to 70,000 sparks per minute for high revving engines of multi-cylinder type. Now being offered on performance saloon cars such as Jaguars.

**ESTATE:** Type of car body which resembles a van with windows. Rear passenger seats fold down to provide flat platform for goods carrying.

**EXHAUST GASES:** As the engine is firing, the fuel mixture burns and gases are given off. These are pushed out into the exhaust pipe. Major gases made include steam, nitrogen, and carbon monoxide (which is poisonous if inhaled for any time in confined space).

**FAN:** A type of propeller used to draw air over a radiator to cool the water inside. Also used to force air over engine parts in air-cooled engine. The fan often has a pulley attached and a belt which drives a water pump and also the generator.

**FASTBACK BODY:** Type of body such as Scimitar GT and Capri Mk 2 and other cars with extended roof line and very little boot. A sleek, sloping rear window shape is synonimous with fast back style.

**FEELER GAUGES:** Accurately made slithers of metal used to set fine tolerances e.g. spark plug gaps, distributor points etc.

**FIBREGLASS:** Wrongly-used term intended to mean GLASS REINFORCED PLASTICS. ("Fibreglass" is, in fact, a manufacturer's trademark).

**FIRING SEQUENCE:** The order in which engine's cylinders operate to give balance e.g. from the front of the engine, No 1 cylinder may be followed by No 3, then No 4 and finally No 2 cylinder.

**FLASHER SWITCH:** Commonly meaning flashing turn indicators but properly meaning a lever which will momentarily flash main beam lights as a signal to another driver.

**FLASHER UNIT:** A switch or nowadays a steering column stalk which operates the turn indicators at front and rear of the vehicle. When in the turn right or turn left position a clicking sound warns the driver that flashers are operating. When road wheels straighten the stalk automatically cancels the flasher.

**FLYWHEEL:** A massive metal disc attached to the engine's crankshaft which absorbs uneven motion caused by the piston's movements.

**FOOTBRAKE:** The car's main braking system is operated by a foot pedal.

**FOUR-WHEEL DRIVE:** Where power is distributed to all four road wheels instead of the normal two. Gives extra grip in difficult conditions such as mud, sand or snow.

**FRICTION PADS:** Pads covered with a special friction-bearing material which are pinched against the revolving disc of disc brake system.

**FRONT WHEEL DRIVE:** Where the engine drives the front wheel as in BLMC Minis, 11/1300 Variants.

**FUEL CELLS:** Normally associated with the chemical storehouse which produces power for electric-motor cars.

**FULL LOCK:** Using the steering wheel to turn the steering wheels to their maximum turn position gives the vehicle "full lock".

**GASKET:** Thin piece of copper and asbestos used to make a gasket and watertight joint between two metal faces.

**GEARBOX:** An assembly of toothed gears which the driver can select via the gear lever to enable the car to produce enough torque for moving off and then progress through to cruising speed.

**GENERATOR:** See Dynamo.

**HANDBRAKE:** A lever beside the driver which operates the rear brakes for parking and to prevent rolling back or forward while waiting.

**HARD-TOP CAR:** Normally applies to a sports car's detachable roof of a solid type.

**GLASS REINFORCED PLASTICS:** Abreviated to g.r.p. Used to build specialist car bodies and comprising glass fibre matting and rovings and resins. 'Fibreglass' is one g.r.p. manufacturer's trademark.

**GRAN TOURISMO:** or sometimes Grand Tourer (shortened to G.T.) Many popular saloons have pepped-up engines to give better performance — but these terms originally applied to luxury, high-powered cars.

**GRILLE:** The front of the car, normally decorative only and with bright metal look.

**HEADLAMPS:** The car's main front lights. One unit now normally contains both main and dipped lights.

**H.T. LEADS:** High tension leads are heavily insulated electrical cables, e.g. from the distributor to the spark plugs.

**HIGHWAY CODE:** Rules of the Road prepared for the use of all road users (not only car drivers) available from most Newsagents and book shops. Get one!

**HORSEPOWER:** A convenient way of expressing the power output gained from an engine. The imperial (British measure of horsepower is slightly higher than the metric h.p. Our rating equals the equivalent of 33,000 foot pounds of work per minute.

**HYDROLASTIC:** A name given to suspension systems using fluid and conical rubber springs to provide an interconnected, compensating suspension system. As used by BLMC on later Minis 11/1300 models etc.

**IDLING:** Or tick over. When the engine is running without acceleration.

**IGNITION SYSTEM:** The complete system which enables the driver to start the engine, normally with a key in the dashboard. This brings the battery into operation, the coil, contact breaker, condenser, distributor, starter motor, and the sparking plugs.

**INDEPENDENT SUSPENSION SYSTEM:** Many cars feature independent front suspension, and sometimes rear suspension too. This enables each wheel to move without interference to or from any of the other wheels.

**IN-LINE ENGINE:** An engine layout where all cylinders are arranged in a straight line from front to the rear of the engine.

**INTEGRAL BODY (or UNITARY):** A form of body construction which does not feature a separate chassis.

**JACK:** A piece of equipment used to raise one side of the car, e.g. in order to change wheels.

**JET:** A small part of a carburettor which adjusts fuel flow.

**JUMP LEADS:** A means of connecting two car batteries together to use one to start the other's engine in an emergency. Each lead is of heavily insulated cable with connecting clips at both ends.

**KICK-DOWN:** A facility normally found on automatic transmissions which chooses a lower gear for improved acceleration on fully depressing the accelerator.

**KNOCK-ONS:** A slang expression for sports wheels which were tightened by turning a large winged nut in the centre.

**LABOURING ENGINE:** Applies when the driver has chosen too high a gear in relation to car speed and the engine finds it difficult to pull the weight.

**LEAF SPRING:** A series of steel strips which are clipped together to form a spring, and are attached to the chassis or car body.

**LIMOUSINE:** A luxury vehicle, normally quite large, which gives the ultimate in privacy and comfort to the occupants. Often chauffeur driven.

**LITRE:** A metric form of measure, e.g. a litre of petrol would be the equivalent to approx. .22 gallon.

**LOG BOOK:** Every car is issued with a Log Book which shows present and previous owners and details of engine and chassis numbers, colour, engine c.c. rating and so on. May be abolished soon, and computerised.

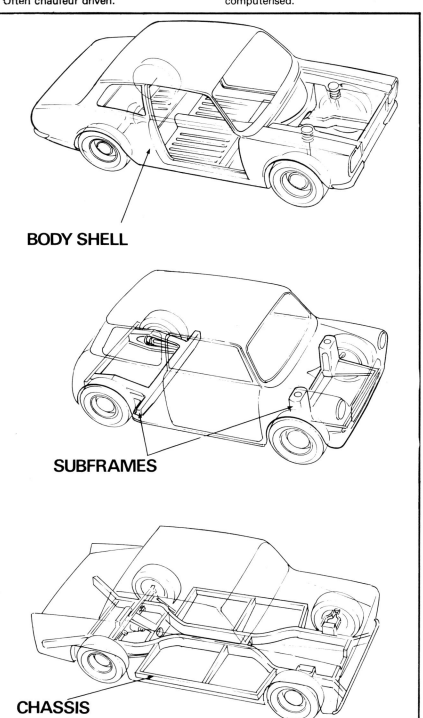

**BODY SHELL**

**SUBFRAMES**

**CHASSIS**

**LUBRICANT**: Oils and grease are lubricants which can be placed between two surfaces to minimise friction.

**MacPHERSON**: Type of Suspension incorporating a damper. Common on Ford cars.

**MANUAL GEARBOX**: A gearbox whereby the driver has to choose the gears himself by using a lever.

**MILEOMETER**: see ODOMETER.

**MONOCOQUE BODY**: A one-piece body construction

**MoT TEST**: Annual test for vehicles over three years old. Now controlled by the DoE (Dept. of the Environment).

**MULTIGRADES**: Oils whose viscosity is more stable due to its make up.

**NEUTRAL**: With the engine running but with no gear engaged to turn the road wheels, a car is said to be in neutral.

**NUMBER PLATE**: Metal plates attached to both front and rear of cars and motorcycles. The plate can be black with white letters and numbers or of the approved safety reflective type with serial identifications on a white background (to front) and a yellow background (to rear). Only cars of the Royal Mews are exempted from carrying number (or licence) plates.

**OCTANE VALUE**: A way of numerically expressing the anti-knock properties of petrol. The higher the number (e.g. 100 octane) the better it should prove for high compression engines.

**ODOMETER**: or Mileometer. A rotating adding-up machine which records the miles travelled by the car. Sometimes a Trip Meter is also included enabling a recording of individual journeys to be made.

**OIL PUMP**: A pump which forces oil around the engine. Some cars have an oil pressure gauge fitted to the instrument panel to tell the driver if anything goes wrong.

**OTTOS's CYCLE**: The originator of the 4-stroke cycle to which our engines today bear much association.

**OVERDRIVE**: An additional gear which, at the flick of a switch, can be brought into play for high speed cruising e.g. on motorways.

**OVERHEAD CAM**: Term used when the engine camshaft is mounted above the cylinder head and operates overhead valves, via tappets or rocker arms. Abbreviations ohc (overhead camshaft) and ohv (overhead valve) are often seen in specifications and magazine articles.

**PETROL**: Made up of light and volatile "hydrocarbon" materials produced from distillation of crude oil (petroleum).

**PETROL INJECTION**: A method which eliminates carburettors and meters the required amount of petrol to the injectors where it is squirted into the combustion chambers.

**PINKING**: Engine runs unevenly due to wrong fuel, or the fact it is too leanly set.

**PISTON**: An engine component which slides up and down inside the combustion chamber. The piston is driven down by the expansion of the burning fuel/air mixture and transmits its movement to the crankshaft.

**PLUG LEADS**: Heavy, insulated cable which carries high voltages necessary for good sparks at the sparking plugs.

**POINTS**: Metal contacts fitted inside the distributor which form part of the ignition system. Also, the end tips of spark plugs electrodes.

**POTS**: An enthusiast's slang for cylinders.

**PROPELLER SHAFT**: (Prop. shaft). Engine power is taken to the driving axle(s) by a prop shaft which on a front-engine, rear-wheel drive is located under a central hump running for and aft in the floor.

**QUARTER LIGHT**: A small window which can normally be opened for ventilation. Fresh-air ventilation systems have meant that many cars no longer have them fitted (e.g. Ford cars).

**QUARTZ-HALOGEN**: A special lamp type which gives a bright, white light.

**RACK & PINION**: Type of steering mechanism. A pinion at the bottom end of the steering column engages in a toothed rack which moves according to the direction of the pinion's rotation.

**RADIATOR**: Part of the cooling system for engine water. The radiator comprises passages with large surface areas through which the water passes, dissipating heat as it circulates through the radiator.

**REAR-WHEEL DRIVE**: One of the most common transmission forms where power from the engine is taken to the rear wheels which drive the car.

**RETREAD**: A tyre which has worn out may have a new tread worked, when it is sold again as a re-tread. Such tyres are not recommended for high-speed driving.

**REV-COUNTER**: See Tachometer.

**RUNNING-IN**: With a new car, or new engine, speed should be limited until the engine has had a chance to work itself in.

**SEAT BELTS**: Safety devices which strap around driver or passengers and are bolted to a reinforced part of the car's structure. A legal requirement for new cars, and for those under a certain age for MoT tests.

**SILENCER**: A metal casing built into exhaust pipe to reduce the exhaust gases pressure before emmission. This cuts out much of the exhaust's noise.

**SMALL END**: (see Big End).

**SPARK PLUG**: A device capable of emitting a high voltage spark to ignite fuel and air mixture in the combustion chamber of an engine.

**SPEEDOMETER**: (shortened to Speedo') An instrument required by law which indicates the speed the car is travelling.

**STALL**: A car stalls when the engine cuts out.

**STAR GRADES**: A system of star ratings denotes octane rating. The British Standards Institution method is: 2 stars for 90 to 93 octanes; 3 stars 94 to 96 octanes; 4 stars for 97 to 99 octanes; and 5 stars for 100 octane petrol.

**STRAIGHT SIX**: An engine with six cylinders in line. (Also "straight eight" etc.).

**SUMP**: A large "pan" under the crankcase which holds oil for the lubrication system.

**SYNCHROMESH**: A special device which eliminates noisy gear changes by automatically "synchronising" the "mesh" of the gears before engagement.

**TACHOMETER**: An instrument which tells the driver the number of revolutions (per minute) of the engine.

**TAPPETS**: Tappets are normally small metal rods or cylinders which are part of the valve-operating system in the engine.

**TOP DEAD CENTRE**: (t.d.c.) The position of a piston in its cylinder at the top of its stroke.

**TORQUE**: The turning power effected by the pistons on the crankshaft.

**TRANSMISSION SYSTEM**: The mechanical parts by which the engine's power (torque) is delivered to the driving wheels.

**TRANSVERSE LAYOUT**: Engine positioned across the car (east-west layout and used to a large extent by manufactures such as Fiat and BLMC on front-wheel drive cars.

**TWO-STROKE ENGINE**: The cycle gives a power stroke on second stroke of the piston rather than on the fourth stroke as in the Otto and 4-stroke cycles. A mixture of petrol and oil is normally used for two-stroke fuel, where the oil is used for lubrication purposes.

**UNITARY CONSTRUCTION**: As INTEGRAL BODY.

**UNIVERSAL JOINTS**: Joints which are able to move in any direction (Abreviated to UJs).

**VALVES**: Trumpet shaped items which control gas flow into and out of the engine's cylinders. Valves and their associated gear are among the most sensitive of the engine's parts.

**"V"-LAYOUT**: Engine layout with two cylinder banks which are V-eed when looked at on end.

**WANKEL ROTARY ENGINE**: Special engine form which has rotating triangular-shaped rotors instead of pistons.

**WATER-COOLING**: System of cooling engine parts by circulating water. (see also RADIATOR).

**WHEELBASE**: Distance between the centres of front and rear wheels.

**ZEBRA**: A black and white striped crossing over a roadway on which pedestrians have right of way once traversing.

# Getting to know . . .

# INSURANCE

BY THE END of 1975, more than half a million new motorists will have joined the ranks of the 18,000,000 drivers already using Britain's roads. Those who become proud owners of a car for the first time will face what is, even for many more experienced motorists, the complex and often bewildering task of arranging motor insurance.

A new motorist who sets about insuring his car will probably be certain of only one thing — that he must have insurance cover before he can take his vehicle out on the road. How much it will cost, what kind of insurance cover he is able to get and which insurance company he insures with will depend on both driver and car, as well as where he lives and even his occupation.

Our new motorist will probably also be aware that the law merely requires him to have what is called ROAD TRAFFIC ACT cover against claims for death or injury to a third party. Like most other drivers, however, he will realise that the risk of an accident on our crowded roads is a very real one and the cost of repairing even minor damage to a vehicle often considerable so that more protective insurance cover is necessary.

Nearly eighty per cent of car owners opt for a COMPREHENSIVE policy which covers both them and their vehicle in addition to third-party claims. Others choose a more restricted policy, known as THIRD PARTY ONLY, which does not cover the policyholder against damage to his own vehicle.

One of the first decisions our new motorist will have to make is whom he should insure with. Confronted with around a hundred insurance companies all offering policies that differ from one another in some respect, the choice may seem at first an almost impossible one. In the back of his mind, perhaps, will be the nagging memory of recent insurance company failures which left many thousands of drivers without cover virtually overnight.

The best way to go about choosing motor insurance is the safe way. Pick an old-established company, preferably one which is a member of the British Insurance Association (though even the BIA cannot offer a guarantee of security) or a Lloyds syndicate, even if it means paying a little extra for added peace of mind.

Alternatively, a reputable insurance broker can take a great deal of hard work and worry out of arranging insurance. But anyone taking out a policy this way should do so through a member of recognised brokers' association such as the Lloyd's Insurance Brokers' Association or the Corporation of Insurance Brokers.

Members of the Automobile Association and the Royal Automobile Club, however, would do well to take advantage of the advice and assistance which both motoring organisations offer on insurance matters.

Anyone taking out a motor policy for the first time, whether or not they have been insured elsewhere before, should always check that they have the cover they require.

Not every policy, for instance, includes cover against windscreen breakage — even under a Comprehensive insurance policy. If it is planned to tow a caravan, an additional policy may be necessary by cover damage to the caravan itself. If short-term cover is required for car hire in the event of your own car being off the road due to accidental damage, a small additional premium may have to be paid.

Extra cover for passengers carried in the car is now required by law and is automatically included in all motor insurance policies.

As with anything as complex as motor insurance, there are bound to be pitfalls. No matter how well-insured a driver is, he can still break the law or have a claim rejected if he fails to comply with the terms of the policy. Most insurance companies require a car owner to take all reasonable steps to maintain the vehicle in a roadworthy condition and take all reasonable precautions to prevent fire and theft.

Before borrowing a friend's car, check that either the

## Three Essential Insurance Documents

**COVER NOTE:** The newly-insured motorist may receive a cover note to tide him over until his certificate of insurance is prepared. It is evidence that he has the insurance required by law. The cover note is valid for a short period and must be renewed if the certificate is delayed.

**CERTIFICATE OF INSURANCE:** Legal proof that the motorist is insured is provided by the certificate of insurance. It details who can drive, and for what purpose. It must be shown on demand to any police officer (or produced at a police station within five days). It is also needed when renewing vehicle excise licence. If the certificate has not been received a valid cover note (but not the policy) will be satisfactory in both these cases. The certificate should be kept in a safe place and taken with the policyholder if he goes on holiday, but should not be left in the car where it could be used by a car thief to convince the police that he is the owner of the car.

**POLICY:** The only document containing the full terms of the motorist's contract with his insurance company is his insurance policy. Its clauses set out in detail what is covered and what is excluded. Endorsements, which are often added at the end of the policy, should be carefully noted. They are alterations in the cover given by the standard policy. For instance, they may reduce the cover or make the policyholder liable to pay the first £25 of a claim.

owner's insurance policy or your own covers you for use. If you lend your car to someone, make sure first that the person borrowing it has a current driving licence; if it is a provisional licence, will he be supervised? and will the car still be covered by your own insurance?

Equally important, a car should only be used for the purposes stated on the insurance policy. Using a car for business, for instance, when it is only covered for private domestic use invalidates the policy. Any information withheld from the insurance company can also invalidate a policy. If particulars on the original proposal form change, tell the company; if you change your occupation, take part in motor rallies, suffer from a disabling illness, or are convicted of a motoring offence — any of these can, and probably will, affect the policy.

How much a motorist pays for his insurance depends on how likely the insurance company thinks he is to make a claim, and therefore cost them money. In other words, what are the chances of him becoming involved in an accident?

Most companies base their premium on some or all of *seven* factors: The driver's age, his driving record, occupation, what the car is used for, where it is kept, its make and model and its value.

If the premium produced by this method is more than the motorist wishes to pay he can choose to restrict the cover in return for a lower premium.

There are a number of practical ways of cutting insurance costs by reducing the cover. The policyholder can agree to restrict the cover to himself only, although this means that there would be no cover if it became necessary for someone else to take over the driving.

He can also opt to pay the first part, say £15 or £25, of any claim for accidental damage to his own car or the first part of any claim under the policy.

The best way to reduce premiums, under most policies, is to see that you never have to make a claim — in other words, take care of your car, drive carefully and take all possible precautions against fire or theft. Insurance companies usually reward such care with a progressive reduction of premiums as the claim-free period grows, known as a No-Claim Bonus or Discount.

Finally, if you eventually become one of the 800,000 British motorists who take their cars abroad each year you will almost certainly have to get extra cover for foreign travel. For many European countries, an International Motor Insurance Certificate, known as a Green Card, is all you require. In the near future. Common Market countries will no longer require visiting British motorists to have a Green Card. But for those that do, apply for the Green Card to your own insurance company before leaving, giving details of countries to be visited and how long you plan to be away.

# Getting to know . . .

# ROADS and MOTORWAYS

THE FIRST ROADS were made in Britain by ancient man, linking settlements and communities. It was not until after the Roman invasion of the British Isles in AD 43 that the first national network of roads began to develop.

The Romans were the first road builders to use scientific methods. As the highways they built were intended for military traffic, they were straight, paying no heed to easy gradients and often going straight over the top of a hill instead of following the lower ground.

Today, there are 210,000 miles of roads of all kinds in Britain. A glance at a map will show that much of the Roman road network still exists, radiating from cities like London, Salisbury and Winchester.

After the Romans had left the British Isles there was little attempt to extend or improve the existing road system for several centuries. In the late eighteenth and early nineteenth centuries the first turnpikes — roads on which tolls were charged — were built. More and more traffic began to use the roads and eventually, in the late 1880's, the first motor cars began to appear in increasing numbers.

Later, highway authorities were set up to improve roads, and in 1919 the Ministry of Transport, now part of the Department of the Environment, was established. The system of A and B roads was introduced to denote main and secondary routes, and signposting developed.

ROAD NUMBERS AND CLASSIFICATIONS were originally introduced solely for administrative reasons. Road numbers now appear on all official signs for classified roads. Numbered roads, besides helping travellers to find their way, indicated that they were reasonably surfaced — and led somewhere.

Since 1919, roads have been classified A or B, and their numbers have been shown on signposts. The plan for numbering is a simple one; England and Wales is divided into 6 zones, the great national highways forming the boundaries. Zones are numbered clockwise from 1 to 6, centred on London, according to the number of the boundary road. The highways concerned are:

| The Great North Road | A1 | The Bath Road | A4 |
| The Dover Road | A2 | The Holyhead Road | A5 |
| The Portsmouth Road | A3 | The Manchester Road | A6 |

Each zone comprises the area from one of these highways to the next in numerical sequence. For example, Zone 1 is from the Great North Road to the Dover Road and therefore covers the eastern countries of England. Zone 2 is from the Dover Road to the Portsmouth Road and covers Kent, Surrey, Sussex and parts of Hampshire; the other zones are formed in the same way. The best analogy is to consider England and Wales as a clock face with London as the centre and the big hand sweeping clockwise over the zones from road to road.

In general the roads in any zone begin with the zone number, no matter how many figures the number may have. For example, A10, A11 and A12 are all to be found in Zone 1; they lead from London to King's Lynn, Norwich and Great Yarmouth respectively. Class B roads beginning with the figure 1 are also in this zone. Similarly the London-Oxford road, A40, and the Aylesbury-Banbury-Birmingham road, A41 are in Zone 4, and also the class B roads beginning with 4.

Motorway numbers are prefixed by the letter M. The long-distance ones in England and Wales are numbered from 1 to 6. They are:

| | |
| --- | --- |
| M1 London-Yorkshire | M4 London-South Wales Radial |
| M2 Medway Motor Road | M5 Bristol-Birmingham |
| M3 London-Southampton | M6 Birmingham-Preston-Carlisle |

Spurs and motorways lying within the sectors bounded by these main motorways are being given two-figure numbers, the first figure being that of the main motorway; e.g. M50 runs from Ross-on-Wye to the M5 near Bredon. Motorways which are merely by-passes along an existing main road do not have an M number,

## MOTORWAY MILEAGES

| | | | | |
| --- | --- | --- | --- | --- |
| LONDON to DOVER | 72 mls | via | M2 |
| LONDON to FOLKESTONE | 75 mls | via | A.20 (M) |
| LONDON to BRISTOL | 116 mls | | M4 |
| LONDON to SOUTHAMPTON | 77 mls | | M3 |
| LONDON to MANCHESTER | 184 mls | | M1 |
| LONDON to NEWCASTLE | 273 mls | via | M1 & A1(M) |
| LONDON to CARLISLE | 298 mls | via | M1 & M6 |
| LONDON to GLASGOW | 392 mls | via | M1, M6 & M74 |
| LONDON to BRIGHTON | 53 mls | | M23 |
| BRISTOL to CARLISLE | 272 mls | via | M5 & M6 |
| GLASGOW to EDINBURGH | 44 mls | | M8 |
| BRISTOL to HULL | 203 mls | via | M5, M6, M1, M18, M62 |

(Extension to M3 — Lightwater to Sunbury — opened July 11th 1974).

# BRITISH MOTORWAY SYSTEMS

**MAXIMUM ADVISED SPEED**

**LANES CLOSED**

**ROAD CLEAR**

## EMERGENCY WARNING SIGNALS

Usually at two-mile intervals on the central reservation with pairs of alternately flashing lights and illuminated blue panel showing white dots to make up warning signs shown below.

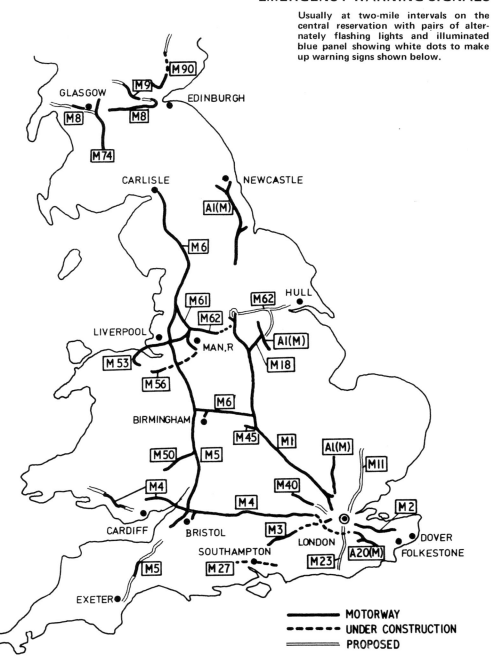

MOTORWAY
---- UNDER CONSTRUCTION
=== PROPOSED

but have the main road number followed by M in brackets; e.g. the Doncaster By-Pass along the A1 is numbered A1(M). This preserves the continuity of the route number of long-distance, all-purpose roads.

Road numbers have yet another important use. With the aid of a map showing them, a motorist can pinpoint his exact position at any signpost showing two or more numbers, as on Salisbury Plain where the road from Amesbury to Wincanton, A303, crossed the Salisbury-Devizes road, A360.

The system of A and B class roads is now no longer officially recognised. Of course, for the convenience of motorists and others who use them, roadside signs have been left and road numbers are still marked on maps. But highway authorities now refer to Trunk Roads (including motorways); Principal Roads (which include most of the A class roads); and Other Roads (including B class and unclassified roads).

Non-motorway trunk roads and all principal roads are known as Primary Routes. These link the primary destinations through the country — more than 350 of them, all important to road traffic and including mostly

towns, but some bridges, tunnels and ferries. Drivers can easily recognise primary routes by their green coloured direction signs at the roadside.

TRAFFIC GROWTH has increased rapidly since the end of the Second World War, while road development has been slow. In 1946 there were just over three million vehicles on the roads in Britain — two thirds of them cars. The number did not increase significantly until the 1950's, but by 1955 there were more than half a million new cars a year registered and the total number of vehicles had reached nearly six and a half million — more than 30 to every mile of road.

Today there are some 16 million vehicles on our roads — 12½ million of them cars — making more than 70 vehicles for every mile of road.

It became clear that a much-improved road network would be required to cope with the growth in the number of cars and other vehicles using the roads. It was from this need that the growth and development of our motorways stemmed.

The first stretch of motorway road to open was the Preston by-pass in December 1958. It ran for 8½ miles along a line now followed by the M.6 which runs north/south through Lancashire.

Nearly a year later, the first stretch of the M.1 opened. The initial section ran for 72 miles between north London and Crick near Rugby. During the first ten years since the M.1 first opened to traffic, its length was extended to 194 miles, and more than 70 million vehicle journeys were made along it.

By the beginning of 1973, there were more than 1,000 miles of motorways throughout Britain. Apart from the ease with which they enable motorists to travel rapidly from one part of the country to another, they are among the safest roads. Carrying five per cent of all traffic, they account for only one per cent of the total number of accidents.

MOTORWAYS differ from other roads in certain important respects. Pedestrians, learner drivers, cyclists and certain types of other vehicles may not use them, for instance.

Most of Britain's motorways are built with three lanes in each direction. The outside (right hand) lane is for overtaking only. Vehicles using the motorway are not allowed to stop except in an emergency (such as a burst tyre or mechanical failure) when they must pull up on the left hand hard shoulder. Everyone must also observe the speed limit of 70 mph, or the limit in force at the time.

**No Cars, No Motor cycles. Any motorist who tried to drive up this narrow, winding footpath in Clovelly, North Devon would need to be a magician!**

Emergency telephones (blue and white or yellow and black) are spaced at intervals of one mile on most stretches of motorway. Marker posts indicating the direction of the nearest telephone are also spaced at intervals of 110 yards along the hard shoulder. The telephones are connected to a motorway control manned by the police who will arrange help if required.

In spite of the fact that motorways are safer than almost all other roads, bad weather can create hazardous driving conditions, especially fog. Warning signals are installed along the motorway to warn drivers of a possible hazard ahead. These are flashing amber lights spaced at intervals along the hard shoulder, although a new computerised signalling system is being installed on some motorways. The new system consists of warning signals at two mile intervals in the centre reservation. When there is danger ahead, amber lights flash and a panel in the centre shows either an advisory speed limit or indicates a lane closure.

On urban motorways, a similar type of computerised signalling is erected overhead every 1,000 yards. In addition to flashing amber lights, panels show the advised maximum speed or arrows point to the lane you should use. When red lights are flashing over your lane, you should stop at the signal.

SIGNS, both on motorways and other roads, are an important part of any road and traffic system. They tell drivers the rules they must keep and warn of what they may meet on the road ahead. Signs may be words and picture symbols on roadside posts, lines and other markings in the road, beacons, bollards or traffic light signals.

Motorway Breakdowns can be a worrying ordeal for a motorist. Alongside the motorway's hard shoulder are sited emergency phones at regular intervals. From these, a motorist will be able to contact the A.A. or R.A.C., or ask for a garage's help if he is not a member. The photographs on the right show one of the many motorway recovery vehicles operated by the A.A. Just under 40 of these ''Hydralifts'' were in service during 1973. The A.A. alone answers over two million calls a year of which many are motorway breakdowns. The Association has 2,000 service aid vehicles on the roads of Britain.

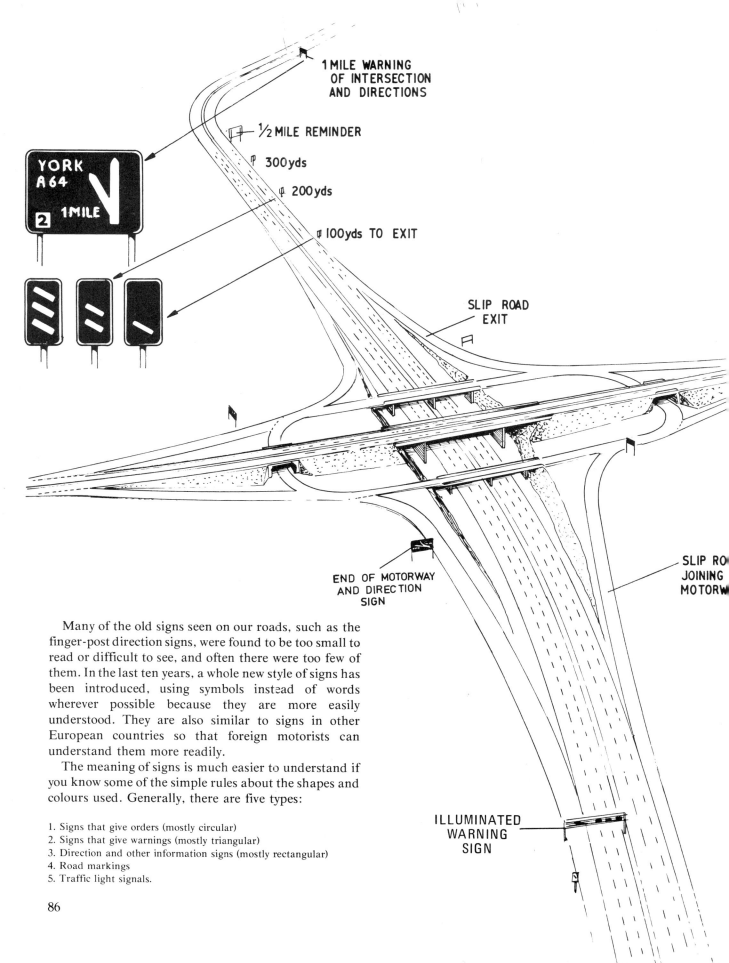

1 MILE WARNING
OF INTERSECTION
AND DIRECTIONS

½ MILE REMINDER

300 yds

200 yds

100 yds TO EXIT

YORK
A64
2 1MILE

SLIP ROAD
EXIT

END OF MOTORWAY
AND DIRECTION
SIGN

SLIP RO
JOINING
MOTORW

ILLUMINATED
WARNING
SIGN

Many of the old signs seen on our roads, such as the finger-post direction signs, were found to be too small to read or difficult to see, and often there were too few of them. In the last ten years, a whole new style of signs has been introduced, using symbols instead of words wherever possible because they are more easily understood. They are also similar to signs in other European countries so that foreign motorists can understand them more readily.

The meaning of signs is much easier to understand if you know some of the simple rules about the shapes and colours used. Generally, there are five types:

1. Signs that give orders (mostly circular)
2. Signs that give warnings (mostly triangular)
3. Direction and other information signs (mostly rectangular)
4. Road markings
5. Traffic light signals.

86

There are also some special signs for motorways. All motorway junctions have numbers to make them easier to identify, the numbers being shown on advance and approach direction signs. Most motorway signs have white lettering on a blue back ground and are much larger than those on ordinary roads so they can be read from a greater distance.

Full details of all British road signs in use are shown in "The Highway Code" available from most newsagents and bookshops, price six pence.

THE RULE OF THE ROAD in Britain is that all traffic should drive on the left. Most other countries, however, keep to the right.

Several possible explanations for this have been put forward. The usual one is that riders on horseback maintained the left because swords were worn on the left and it made sense to keep one's mount to that side of the road. If attacked by highwaymen, the rider was at once in the best fighting position, sword ready in his right hand, with his left side automatically protected.

Napoleon is supposed to have upset this practice by not only attacking from the right flank, but also by adding to the confusion of his enemies by ordering the French troops to march on the righthand side of the road, opposite to the usual direction of traffic!

Another suggestion is that waggoners and coachmen always sat on the right side of their vehicles so they could wield their long whips freely in their right hands without interference from the load behind. When they met another vehicle it was natural to pull over to the left, so that they were in the best position to negotiate the narrow, often slippery roads.

From this habit, it is believed, came the British custom of keeping to the left. On the Continent, however, postillions were more usual and the rider sat astride the left rear horse because this was the best position for controlling the team. As a result, when they encountered one another, they instinctively pulled over to the right in order to gauge the clearance.

Many countries probably used left or right hand fashions indiscriminately until traffic became denser, when it became evident that some rule would have to be adopted if traffic was to move in safety.

Britain's "keep left" rule was not made law until as late as 1835. In recent times, several countries have changed over from driving on the left to driving on the right. The most recent was Sweden in 1967.

Better safe than sorry. This young lady is se[a]
wearing a seat belt. Notice also the padded s[?]
wheel and built-in head restraint to the seat.

# Getting to know . . .

# SAFER MOTORING

"A CAR IS only as safe as its driver" . . . how often have you heard people say that! There is of course a certain amount of truth in this statement; you only have to think of a drunken driver's reactions (or rather lack of them) to understand that there could be something to be said for better driver training and education in special aspects of car control.

But even the most skilful of drivers would find it difficult to stop from 70 miles per hour in a motorway emergency if the car's brakes were inoperative!

A recent United Nations Survey gave specific figures which bring home the fact that a safety-conscious attitude to motoring by every driver would ensure less fatalities on our roads.

The figures of deaths on the roads of Europe have been put at just under 90,000 in just one year. Think of it! And add to that dreadful sum well over *two million* European drivers and passengers who received injuries as a result of car accidents in a similar year.

Accidents are rarely attributable to major mechanical failures in cars. If it is not the car, then it must be the motorist who is at fault. After all, Governments can legislate to improve road safety all they want, but there will always be accidents as long as we have that common factor of human error.

If the problem cannot be cured, what can we and the car makers' safety research boffins try to do to minimise the possibility of bad accidents?

## What can be done to make our cars safer to drive?

There are really four aspects which we can look at.

The first concerns the car's design: it needs to be very stable and be able to stop as well as possible without skidding, and steer well under all driving conditions. This will enable the driver to control the vehicle with greater accuracy and confidence.

The next approach is to try and improve the protection of both the driver and his passengers. This can be achieved by arranging for the car's body panels to absorb the energy in a head-on or rear impact, by strong side panels to doors and the areas surrounding the passengers. Steering wheels can be made to "collapse" away to save the driver from severe injury to the chest, and so on.

Pedestrians, too, are often involved in car accidents and much more work is being put into designing car bonnets and exterior appendages which will present the least possible damage to the poor pedestrian.

The fourth aid to greater motoring safety concerns the roads on which we drive — better surfacing, better signposting of hazards. Careful choice of materials for such fixtures as bollards, lamp posts and barriers are coming. Hit a solidly-built bollard at only 20 miles per hour and severe damage to a car and its occupants can be inflicted. But sit the bollard on a strong but "break-away" foundation, make the bollard itself from a light plastic or even rubber material, and the car will receive less damage and offer everyone a better chance to survive the incident.

## Over to the car builders

So much for what *could* help to give us safer motoring in the future. What can the car makers offer in the way of safety devices built into the cars they are constantly tempting everyone to buy?

Every new car in Britain must, by law, be fitted with strong mountings to take seat belts for both driver and front seat passenger. Some manufacturers are tending to offer their cars fitted with belts at an all-in price to the customer. Others give the buyer choice of type of belt (there are basically two types on the market — static or inertia reel versions). In this case, the "extras" list will show the types available which can be fitted at a small charge.

In all but the worst car crash a seat belt is now given credit as a convenient form of life saver, restraining the driver or his passenger from rocketing through the windscreen and then whiplashing back into his seat only to have his neck broken. Even a driver who does not "belt up" will probably acknowledge the fact that the wearing of a seat belt helps to minimise injury.

Jimmy Saville's "Clunk Click" advertisements during 1972 to 1974 did much to bring home the tragedies of motoring accidents to those motorists who profess that "it could never happen to me". Through his hard, often shocking interviews with crash survivors, Jimmy has done much to educate the driver to wear his seat belt — and in so doing probably encouraged many passengers to join the seat belt brigade.

The fact that you have to make a conscious effort to strap up before driving off has resulted in much research into other "passive restraint" systems. The system which has received a dubious reception is the Air Bag. Until recently, safety experts in United States, the home of safety consciousness, favoured the air bag. But despite its various advantages the systems developed so far have been criticised on various counts. Not least of these is the fact that the operation of the bag, triggered off by a

sensing device at the front or rear end of the vehicle, could suffer from a failure to operate just when required. Secondly, the fact that it can blow up across the driver's field of vision means that he will have very little chance of controlling his car should it still be on the move after an accident!

The air bag principle relies on a specially designed plastic bag which is sited strategically on a car's fascia. The bag is connected to a gas cylinder which in turn is coupled to special switches which are only brought into play when an impact occurs. The impact-sensitive switch actuates the release mechanism on the gas container and — whoosh!

The bag inflates instantly in front of the driver and his passenger, preventing their otherwise inevitable and painful argument with the windscreen and their uncontrollable return to a possible neckbreaking encounter with their seats again.

Making a convenient package of an air bag restraint system and concealing its presence in as unobtrusive position as possible has taxed many a safety research team. One system even sites individual air bags for each

*(Continued on page 91)*

More than 100 emergency stops are made during a Ford anti-skid test, with speeds up to 70 mph in conditions simulating dry, damp, wet and icy roads. During each test a mini computer stores information on wheel speed, deceleration, stopping distance and other vital data.

Cars can be "crushed" in slow motion. At any stage of the impact, engineers can stop the crash to examine what is happening to the car. This rig used by Ford Motor Company crushes a Capri into a barrier at the rate of half-an-inch per second. This simulates what happens when a car would crash at 30 mph.

# CRUSHING

# ...and CRASHING

This ten-second spectacular was part of another Ford safety research programme. The driver, a stock car racing driver, offered his services as a test driver to determine what actually happened to people inside a car during a nasty accident!

of the front seat occupants. The passenger's is neatly camouflaged into the fascia while the driver's is concealed in the hub which forms the centre of the steering wheel.

## Other restraint systems

Other suggestions have been researched such as padded arms which, on opening the car door, retreat to allow the driver to get seated — but on closing the door the restraining arm automatically positions itself across the seat's occupant.

Other systems are based on the latest seat belt types which are reasonably inexpensive to install (about a quarter of the cost of fitting the air bag system for which buyers of American Chevrolets pay about £80). It is relatively easy to prevent a motorist from starting his car and moving off if he is not wearing his seat belt. The system which does not allow the ignition key to be turned until the seat belt has been put on would seem to be a straightforward and generally acceptable way of reminding the driver of his own, and others' safety. A

system using ultrasconics has been developed by one major manufacturer and cuts out any chances of a driver sabotaging the system by sitting on his belt, fastening it around the back of his seat — or even cutting off the buckle!

## Other aspects of safety

The United States of America have become renowned for their stringent, some may even say impractical, requirements for vehicle safety controls.

All cars sold in the United States of America are subject to the legal requirements set down by the National Highway Traffic Safety Administration which was set up over a decade ago to stipulate what safety requirements should be met by car makers, and to enforce the standards they set.

America may sound a long way off, but the effect of its safety legislation is naturally felt by any manufacturer anywhere in the world who wishes to maintain car sales in the USA. Because of this, most manufacturers have devoted countless man-hours and money developing

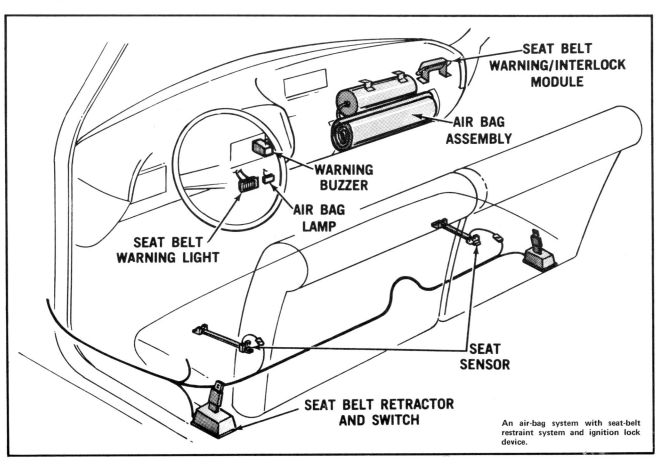

SEAT BELT WARNING/INTERLOCK MODULE

AIR BAG ASSEMBLY

WARNING BUZZER

AIR BAG LAMP

SEAT BELT WARNING LIGHT

SEAT SENSOR

SEAT BELT RETRACTOR AND SWITCH

An air-bag system with seat-belt restraint system and ignition lock device.

improvements to their vehicles' safety specifications for inclusion not only in vehicles exported to American buyers, but also in the makers' home territories.

On the home and European front standards are many and various though member countries of the Common Market are beginning to standardise their requirements.

## From hinges to "drunkometers"

The most important standards cover such design points as the requirements for doorlocks to be burst-proof, the design of door hinges, impact-collapsable steering columns, and steering wheels, and so on.

Exhaust emission control has been another goal for the manufacturers' scientists as has the controlled crushability of energy-absorbing body panels.

There are moves afoot to increase the range of standards to cover interior padding for improved passenger protection, for the further reduction in pollution caused by exhaust fumes, and for many other aspects of safety which, if the manufacturers can cope, will bring safer, cleaner motoring.

The Americans' standards are, indeed, far more

Saab 99 EMS Saloon.

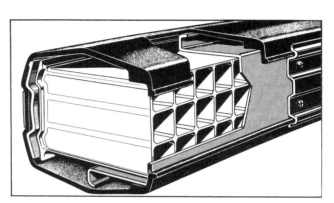

. . . the bumper in action

comprehensive and cover such things as built-in head rests (head restraints) to cut the chances of a motorist having his neck snapped should someone decide to drive into his car's back end.

From 1976 American-sold cars must have the safety belt/ignition lock device mentioned earlier. The requirement might also call for warning lights, and perhaps buzzers to remind drivers (and their front seat passenger) that someone has not belted up.

There has even been the suggestion that a specially designed instrument affectionately known as a "drunko-meter" should be installed to combat drunken drivers causing havoc on roads and motorways.

With this natty gadget, the car's ignition key cannot be turned until the driver proves his reactions are up to par by completing an electronic puzzle within a specified time. If he doesn't—he just has to sit and sober up. The only problem with this is that if a person is going to be irresponsible enough to drive while "under the influence" he will probably be the type to jot down the puzzle's solution for reference!

Other American safety requirements involve no small expense by the motor manufacturers; for example, crash testing vehicles to ensure that the standards for each

The 99 has built-in seat head restraints . . .

. . . a headlamp cleaning system.

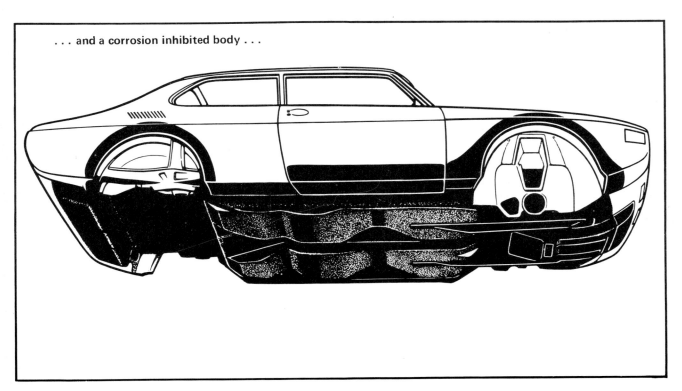
. . . and a corrosion inhibited body . . .

model being sold in the United States are being met. Ford Motor Company alone crashed 500 vehicles in one year to prove the point that the model came up to scratch.

American cars also have to have bumpers fitted that are designed to absorb, and withstand, an impact of five miles per hour.

## Non-skid braking systems

Imagine the confidence a driver would have if he knew his car would not skid in an emergency stop! How often have you seen a motorist thump on "the anchors" only to waltz ungraciously out of control instead of coming to a sudden, straight-line halt?

Lucas' headlamp wiper system.

Car manufacturers' research teams, such as those from Mercedes Benz and the Volvo Company, have been investigating the possibilities of a non-skid braking system for some years now, as have British companies including names like Dunlop and Girling. But despite set-backs in producing a fool-proof system at a realistic cost to the car buyer, it looks as if new research into the problem of skid control could come to fruition soon. There are systems available for lorries (especially articulated ones where braking can often cause the trailer to "jack knife" out of control) and these have been incorporated on rather expensive cars like the now obsolete Jensen.

## Clean bright lights

We have windscreen wipers to improve our vision through the windscreen — so why not fit wipers to a car's headlamps to keep them shining clean and bright? Add

a washer and the filth and grime thrown up from the road can be wiped clear giving improved chances to the driver of seeing what is in front of him at night. Volvo was one of the first manufacturers to fit such equipment as a standard feature — on the 164 TE saloon.

Other bright ideas being looked into included headlamps which can see round corners, such as those fitted by the French Citroen company. As the driver turns, say, to the right, the gearing to the headlamp assemblies swivel to aim the beam in the same direction.

Rear lights have also come up for some debate in recent years — are they bright enough in daytime when road conditions are hazardous (e.g. in fog or snow) . . . are they easily seen at night but not so bright as to dazzle the driver behind? Lights with a choice of two intensities to cope with day and night driving are becoming obligatory in many European countries, hazard warning lighting (which operates all direction indicators) is also becoming obligatory.

And have you ever been a passenger in a car when suddenly, from around a corner, comes another vehicle with such bright lights that you have been blinded? The driver next to you may try to flash his main beam to warn the other motorist that his vision is being impaired by, perhaps, the main beam lights of the oncoming car only to find that the other car flashes his main beam back!

It must be then, that the guilty car has his dipped beam set at too high an angle. Estate cars and vans are often culprits in this respect. Unloaded, the lights may be just right for night driving but with a full load in the back of the car, the front end points the lamps more into the night air.

One way over this would be to fit cars with lamps whose beams can be adjusted to suit the rear end load. It is rumoured that the German Transport Ministry will be initiating laws to cover this important safety point in about 1977. Initially, the German authorities may allow manually operated devices to be used such as that developed by the Bosch company which uses a hydraulic plunger operated by a dashboard-mounted knob and connected to the headlamps' reflectors by plastic tubing. A fluid in the tubing transmits the movement of the plunger and so adjusts the position of the reflectors.

More sophisticated versions will also be available which use special transmitters linked to the front and rear suspensions. These measure the position of the vehicle under different loadings and the headlamps are automatically adjusted by a similar hydraulic principle to the one just mentioned. This way, the headlamp beams should always present themselves at the best position for the driver of the car, and being always correctly aligned should cut down dazzle to oncoming motorists.

This Jaguar 4.2 saloon has had a "blow-out" at 80 mph, but the Avon Safety Wheel allows the car to be brought to a safe stop.

## And what of tyres

In another chapter we discuss tyres as they have been, as they are today, and as they may be in the future.

The latest developments in tyre manufacture and safety came with the 1973 introduction of Dunlop's Denovo tyre which, if punctured, can be "run flat" at 50 mph for up to 100 miles.

Other tyres offer similar safety-plus points, but Dunlop were the first to put such a safety tyre on the market.

The Denovo is fitted to a special wheel which stops the tyre falling off the rim when being run after a puncture. Friction from the flat tyre passes heat to a special liquid — and a gas is given off which then partially reinflates the injured rubber.

Competition has come from the Avon company whose safety wheel design is claimed to be less costly, and simpler in concept. The idea behind Avon's tyre is similar to the Denovo — to keep the tyre on the rim and allow the motorist to get to his nearest garage for repairs to be carried out. Unfortunately the Avon safety tyre is not reckoned to give the driver as much control of his car after a puncture as the Denovo, though enough to bring the car safely out of what would otherwise be a potentially dangerous situation.

Pirelli, well-known Italian tyre manufacturers have also put in a heavy research programme on producing a safety tyre with much success. However, Pirelli is still trying to improve its own design.

## What other safety features could we use?

There are many and various ways in which to improve car safety — or at least cut down potential injury to anyone involved in an accident. Let's take the interior of a modern car and see what the manufacturers and owners can try to achieve.

First, we have talked about passenger restraint systems such as seat belts. Once again, Volvo impress upon us the importance of wearing a seat belt:

"55 per cent of all fatalities would have escaped serious injury had they been wearing a seat belt". "In 28,000 accidents investigated (**in Sweden**) there was not one single fatality in crashes at speeds below 100 kilometres per hour (60 miles per hour) when the seat belt was in use.

Transistors for comfort! This mirror automatically deflects the glare from following vehicles' headlights. A photo-resistive cell and transistors control the mechanism which moves the mirror.

An underbonnet view of the first Lucas radar transmission and receiving horns. On the right — the later version which has miniaturised the system to a size not much larger than a headlamp mounted in the middle of the grille.

And if such good can come from the front seat passenger wearing their seat belts, should we not also fit belts for the rear seat occupants? It has been proved under test that a rear seat passenger, thrown forward by an impact with another car, can cause serious injury to his front seat friends if not kept in place by a belt.

But back to the driver's seat. What can be done to minimise injury? Well, what about the steering wheel? This should be very well padded to absorb impact as the driver's chest hits it. The steering column should also be energy absorbing in the event of a more serious crash, allowing for a "crumple" zone in the steering wheel's mounting, as well as half-way down the steering column itself.

Then there are items such as door handles and window winders which could be recessed into door panels, out of harm's way — as Triumph has been doing for many years on their 1500 saloons (and now on the many variants such as Toledo and others).

One of the nastiest appendages which can catch the driver or passengers' heads is the interior rear-view mirror. The mirror is normally screwed into the roof. Now if the mirror and its stalk was easy to break off, as soon as a passenger collided with it, less injury would be done — and a replacement interior mirror with such a safety-minded design would cost only a pound or so.

Removing one nasty item like a mirror, and replacing it with a safer device is fine. But if the driver hits the windscreen itself then his forward momentum will push his head straight through the glass.

## Laminations save lamentations

A great deal of experiment has been carried out by the manufacturers of windscreens and by the Transport & Road Research Laboratory into the best type of screen.

The regular "toughened" glass type seems fine to look through but is extremely dangerous when an accident happens as the driver's or front seat passenger's head smashes the screen, and passes through the shattered glass. As the momentum is lost, the unfortunate's head and body then return to the inside of the car — the head being dragged across the splinters of glass remaining in the grip of the window rubber.

The best solution so far has seemed to be to fit a "laminated" windscreen made up of two layers of glass material sandwiching a layer of plastics. This type of screen does not shatter like the toughened glass versions, but merely crazes as the driver's head hits it and pushes its more pliable form outwards.

Though more costly than toughened glass, it would seem that laminated screens are a marvellous investment — although not 100% insurance against injury and possible death.

## Rolling over

The anti-roll bar, a common "extra" fitted to soft top sports cars, rally cars and to some saloons, prevents the car's roof from crushing in the event of the car turning over. Combined with a strengthed passenger compartment (e.g. with stress members in doors fitted with anti-burst locks etc.) the roll-over bar can be the final touch in providing a strong passenger compartment able to give the passengers as much of a survival chance as possible.

## Bumpers and Dodgems

One of the American safety standards requires cars sold in the USA to be able to withstand, without damage, impact at low speed — say 5 miles per hour. If all cars could be fitted with good, strong bumpers at both front and rear (and at a standard height!) we would be getting somewhere.

If the bumpers could also be energy absorbing, and able to take small impacts without damage, we would be well on the way to cutting out very minor accidents. Once again, the Swedish car-maker Volvo has been one of the leaders in Europe and Scandinavia. In 1974 models they introduced a bumper design which involved the use of shock-absorbing mountings to absorb initial crash impact and give complete protection at "parking" speeds up to about 5 miles per hour. (Page 92).

But what of "dodgems"? If you have ever been in a car as a passenger when the poor driver has had to drive in thick fog — a real "pea souper" — then you will know how much concentration he has to give to his driving, dodging around parked cars which suddenly appear out of the mist, or avoiding a car which jumps out of the fog and wants to turn across his path.

Back in October 1972, the Lucas company, one of the largest suppliers of electrical equipment to the British motor industry, introduced prototypes of their "Radar Headway Control". A year later, in 1974, the firm showed how research had miniaturised the radar system to the size of a headlamp by fitting the system to a Triumph car's grille (pictures opposite).

Once again, this futuristic device has come about by suggestions that the United States National Highway Traffic Safety Administration will be envisaging such a system being included in future legislation.

The radar system is intended automatically to adjust both brake and throttle controls in order to keep cars at a safe, predetermined distance from the vehicle in front and thereby cut down motorway pile-ups and the hazards of driving in fog.

The Lucas system comprises a flat plate aerial, which receives a signal from the presence of a vehicle in front of it. A digital micro-computer is used to calculate from the radar beam's signals exactly what the brakes and throttle should be doing in order to keep at a safe distance.

If found to be acceptable to the public, the makers feel that it should be possible to introduce a radar signal device of this type within about five years. And the cost? They reckon that it should cost no more than a good car radio.

## Standard safety features . . .

There are many safety features which can be built into the car of today, and which ought to be built into cars of the future. Volvo has been mentioned several times here, and they have a very good record in this field. Their achievements in fitting items as standard on their cars (see table below) are something of a challenge to other manufacturers.

### Dates of Important Volvo Safety Features

|  |  |
| --- | --- |
| 1944 | Laminated Screen |
| 1956 | Safety Steering Column with Shear Coupling |
| 1958 | Rear Seat Belt Anchorages |
| 1959 | Front seat Belts Fitted on production cars |
| 1962 | Disc Brakes |
| 1965 | Brake Servo and Pressure-Limiting Valve (Rear) |
| 1966 | Dual Circuit Fail-Safe Braking |
| 1966 | Anti-Burst Door locks |
| 1966 | Roll-Over Bar in Roof |
| 1968 | Impact-Absorbing Body with Galvanised Floor Sections |
| 1969 | Head Restraints (Front) |
| 1969 | Heated Rear Screen |
| 1970 | Rear Washer/Wiper for Estate Cars |
| 1971 | "Fasten Seat Belt" Warning Light |
| 1973 | Side Impact Members in Doors |
| 1973 | Crumple-Zone in Steering Head |
| 1974 | Shock-Absorbing Bumpers |
| 1974 | Impact-Absorbing Steering Column |
| 1974 | Audio-Visual Seat Belt Reminder |
| 1974 | Fuel-Tank Protected from Rear Impact |

# THE MOTOR SPORT SCENE TODAY

BELIEVE IT OR not the first real motor race was held as long ago as 1895! It ran from Paris to Bordeaux and back, a distance of some 732 miles, and the winner, a gentleman named Levassor, took 48 hours 48 minutes to complete the course to average just 15 mph. Levassor drove a French Panhard car which had a 1,200 cc twin-cylinder engine developing a rousing 4 horse-power! Today a typical Formula One Grand Prix will be held on a specially-built closed circuit over a distance of about 200 miles. The winner will take less than two hours to complete the race and his car will have a 3-litre engine with eight or twelve cylinders producing over 460 horse-power. Times have changed and since Levassor's victory at the very dawn of motoring motor sport has grown into a vast and complicated industry which spans the whole world.

Of course racing is just one of the many activities which together are given the label "motor-sport". In addition to pure racing there is rallying, rally-cross, hill climbs, drag-racing, auto-cross and sprints to name but a few. Each branch of the sport demands its own particular skills and techniques on the part of the driver and, in most cases, demands its own particular type of car.

Like most other sports, motor-sport has its rules and has an international governing body, the Federation Internationale de l'Automobile (FIA) which has its headquarters in Paris. The FIA controls the sport through the national automobile clubs of all the various countries (in Great Britain, for example, the RAC) and stipulates which types of car can be used in the various events, the form which different motor-sports shall take, and so on. In fact, each branch of motor-sport has its own rules which are designed to ensure as far as possible that the drivers are competing on equal terms. Also the rules are aimed at making the sport as safe as possible, that the drivers are competing on equal terms, and cars and circuits have to conform to certain safety standards for the protection of both drivers and spectators alike.

On the surface, the subject of rules may seem dull and uninteresting, yet it is the rules of any sport which decide the form it shall take. Football would be a very different game is eight players instead of 11 made up a team or if there was no offside rule. Tennis would not be the same if the server was allowed only one service instead of two, or if the net was three inches lower. The same is true of motor-sport and the rules are being constantly examined to find out if they should be changed.

## The formula formulae

Of all motor-sport activities it is probably motor racing that is best known and races are held for all types of car imaginable. Basically, cars used for racing can be divided into three main categories, single-seaters, sports cars and saloons. Each category is itself further sub-divided into individual formulae, groups or classes. If we take the single-seaters, pure racing cars with cigar-shaped bodies and exposed wheels, we find that they are split up into Formula One, Formula Two, Formula Three, and a host of others besides.

Formula One is the Grand Prix formula, the type of racing best-known to the public at large, and the formula which produces drivers like Juan Manuel Fangio, Stirling Moss, Graham Hill and Jackie Stewart whose names are household words everywhere. It is the Formula One cars and drivers who compete each year for the World Championship of Drivers, the greatest honour in motor-sport. Races in the Championship are held in countries all over the world including the Argentine, Brazil, Canada, South Africa and the USA as well as in the more traditional European states.

The cars themselves have to be single-seater racing cars with the wheels mounted outside the body. Engines are limited to a maximum of 12 cylinders and can be of up to a capacity of 3 litres unsupercharged or 1½ litres if a supercharger is fitted. So far all the various makers of Formula One engines such as BRM, Ferrari, Ford, Matra, Tecno and Weslake have opted for 3-litres unsupercharged, nobody having elected to make a supercharged 1½ litre power unit. A minimum weight limit of 575 kilogrammes is imposed and among the many other regulations is one limiting the maximum

*Continued on page 105*

## Formula One: TYRRELL-FORD 005

This Tyrrell-Ford Formula One Car has a mid-engined, rear-wheel drive layout. (The engine is a Ford V8 of 3-litre capacity). The chassis is constructed of light alloy with an integral fabricated steel frame at the front.

Dimensions are: Wheelbase 94.05 ins. Track 63.0 ins. front, 62.9 - 64.9 ins. rear, depending on the wheel rim width used. Overall length 146 ins. Overall height 40 ins. to top of intake duct. Ground clearance 3.30 ins. fully laden. Independent suspension to front and rear.

Steering is by rack and pinion with a steering wheel 11 ins. in diameter.

Instruments include tachometer, oil pressure and temperature, water temperature and fuel pressure.

Brakes are Girling hydraulic type with light alloy calipers and 10.5 diameter discs.

A Hewland five-speed gearbox, twin plate Borg & Beck clutch. GKN constant velocity drive shafts make up the transmission.

The nose moulding, cockpit-fairing, oil radiator and air intake ducts are resin bonded glass fibre reinforced with carbon fibre. (Nose unit fitted with adjustable flaps for downthrust variation). Rear wing constructed of light alloy with adjustable flaps and mounted on the gearbox.

Petrol is contained in three cells within the body. Fuel capacity 41 gallons.

Wheels are made of cast magnesium alloy. Tyres are Goodyear.

Safety: A self-contained Graniver BCF fire extinguishing system is fitted for safety. Operation is by the driver or by heat sensing switches.

1890 LUTZMAN HORSELESS CARRIAGE

# The Leaders

Cars that have caught the imagination of the enthusiasts over the years

1911— MODEL T FORD TRUCK
(VALUE TODAY — APPROX £2,000)

1902 — PANHARD LEVASSOR, 10 HP,
2 CYLINDER (VALUE TODAY — APPROX £5,000)

1925 — 3 LITRE BENTLEY VANDEN PLAS TOURER

1921 — ROLLS ROYCE SILVER GHOST
40/50 HP TORPEDO TOURER
(VALUE TODAY APPROX £10,000)

1928 — BUGATTI 3 LITRE TOURER

1929 — VERNON-DERBY 1100cc SPORTS
(COPY OF FRENCH AMILCAR)

1931 — ENGINE DETAIL OF 1931 ALFA
ROMEO ZAGATO 8 CYLINDER
(SUPERCHARGED)

1931 — LAGONDA 2 LITRE (SUPERCHARGED)

1932 — MORGAN FITTED WITH 8 HP JAP ENGINE

102

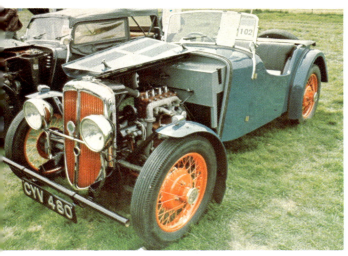

1936 — BSA SCOUT 9 HP, 4 CYLINDER

1937 — MORRIS 8 HP 4-SEAT TOURER

1952 — MG TD 1250 cc 2-SEAT SPORTS

1953 — MORRIS MINOR 948 cc TOURER

1959 — Mk 1 AUSTIN-HEALEY SPRITE (FROGEYE)

1967 — ROLLS ROYCE SILVER SHADOW 6.9 LITRE

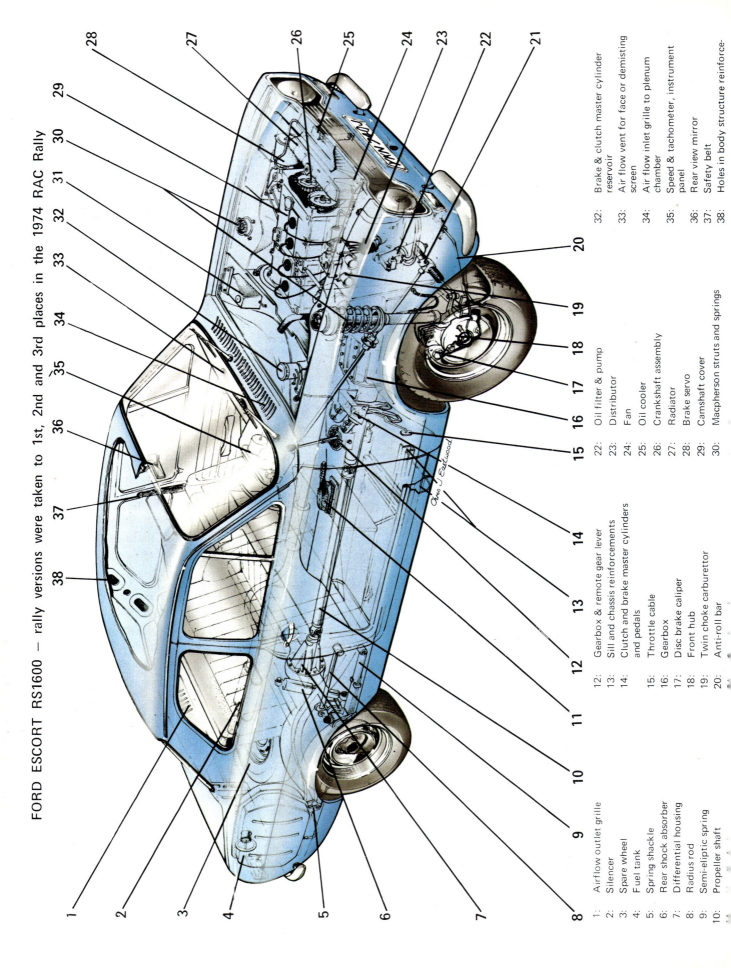

FORD ESCORT RS1600 — rally versions were taken to 1st, 2nd and 3rd places in the 1974 RAC Rally

1: Airflow outlet grille
2: Silencer
3: Spare wheel
4: Fuel tank
5: Spring shackle
6: Rear shock absorber
7: Differential housing
8: Radius rod
9: Semi-elliptic spring
10: Propeller shaft

12: Gearbox & remote gear lever
13: Sill and chassis reinforcements
14: Clutch and brake master cylinders and pedals
15: Throttle cable
16: Gearbox
17: Disc brake caliper
18: Front hub
19: Twin choke carburettor
20: Anti-roll bar

22: Oil filter & pump
23: Distributor
24: Fan
25: Oil cooler
26: Crankshaft assembly
27: Radiator
28: Brake servo
29: Camshaft cover
30: Macpherson struts and springs

32: Brake & clutch master cylinder reservoir
33: Air flow vent for face or demisting screen
34: Air flow inlet grille to plenum chamber
35: Speed & tachometer, instrument panel
36: Rear view mirror
37: Safety belt
38: Holes in body structure reinforce-

The Capri RS 2600 was introduced by Ford to touring car racing circuits in 1973. With a top speed of 174 mph and an engine developing 320 brake horsepower the RS 2600 we see here is a far cry from the Capris we see on the road: front spoiler gives better road grip, and an air induction fuel-injected V-6 engine, glass fibre wheel arches, "fat" tyres etc. all help to give a weight of 2,034 lb.

. . . and this is the fuel-injected V6 power plant which takes her up to that 174 mph. In November 1973 Ford took Capri one stage further — with the RS3100 road car. The Capri Mk 2 range was introduced in 1974, but RS3100 still keeps the Mk 1 shape.

amount of fuel to be carried to about 55 gallons. FIA regulations governing international championships stipulate that only normal pump petrol can be used and so the cars run on the same sort of fuel you can buy at your local garage. Special "dope" fuels containing alcohol and other power-boosting ingredients are banned. Even so a Grand Prix car is phenomenally fast and, depending on the circuit, regularly achieves speeds in excess of 180 mph.

Naturally these cars are very expensive both to build and to run. An engine alone can cost £7,500 and it's essential to have a spare motor on hand in case of a blow-up. Add to this the cost of the car itself, spares, a transporter and all the other hundred-and-one things needed to put the car on the track and you can easily see how the bill for a season's Grand Prix racing can top the £150,000 mark by a very handsome margin.

## Formula Two

The other type of single-seater racing in which the Grand Prix drivers regularly take part is Formula Two. In this formula the cars are simpler and smaller than their Grand Prix brothers and have 2-litre engines which have to use the cylinder block of a production engine of which at least 1,000 have been made. Non-standard cylinder heads may be fitted but only if at least 100 of these special heads have been made and their production registered with the FIA. Despite these strict rules, Formula Two engines develop over 280 horse-power and provide close, exciting racing. While being another form of racing in which the stars can use all their skills, Formula Two also serves as a very useful stepping stone for the younger, less-experienced drivers to graduate to the really big time.

## Formula Three

Essentially an "apprentice" formula, Formula Three is again a single-seater formula, but for cars powered by a 1,600cc engine fitted to a normal car of which at least 5,000 are made each year. Considerable modifications are allowed to be made to these engines, but the power that can be obtained is limited by an additional regulation which states that all the air going into the engine must pass through a single hole 21.5mm in diameter.

No mention of single-seater racing cars would be complete without reference to the cars used in that most famous of American races, the Indianapolis 500. "Indy" is in fact but one event in an American Championship series organised by the United States Auto Club (USAC).

In general layout the cars resemble Formula 1 machines being rear-engined open-wheelers, though they are considerably longer and generally more massive. However, this superficial similarity ends with the engine. Most popular "mill" for the USAC Championship projectiles is the 2.6 litre, 4-cylinder Offenhauser unit, the design of which originated in the 1930's. But don't let that fool you. The current version develops nearly 900 bhp or getting on for double the power of an F1 unit! The power is produced by the combination of highly-potent alcohol-based fuel and the fact that the engines are turbocharged. Turbochargers were used extensively by World War II military aircraft and are a form of supercharger where the fuel and air mixture is forced into the engine by a blower driven by the engine's exhaust gasses.

Sports car racing was originally for road-going sports cars on sale to the general public and its history is studded with names like Alfa-Romeo, Aston-Martin, Bentley, Lagonda, Mercedes-Benz, M.G., Sunbeam and so on. But today the World Championship of Makes, as the big sports-car series is known, is for highly-specialised vehicles owing more to Formula 1 cars than to cars used on the roads. (continued on page 108)

**The 1974 Chevrolet Camaro Z28 — sporty for saloon car racing.**

# THE THINGS THEY DO TO HELP US!

Win a race and the glory is the winner's. But that glory also rubs off onto the car and its manufacturer. Here we see just how one car, the Escort, is sacrificed for the glory of everyone associated with the name. But for all that, valuable information on engineering, comfort and safety is fed back into the design so that, in the end, every motorist is the winner.

**Top Right:** Hanny Mikkola and Gunnar Palm speed their way to Mexico in the 1970 World Cup Rally.

**Centre Right:** And again they set the pace on the Safari-Rally in an Escort RS1600.

**Bottom Right:** Rally Cross (or "snow-cross"?)

**Left:** RS1600 in the 1973 Monte Carlo Rally. 1974 saw three RS1600s take top places in the RAC Rally over 2,000 miles.

Most of the chief contenders for the Championship such as Ferrari, Matra and Mirage all have basically Formula 1 engines which, however, are tuned for reliability rather than maximum power. The cars have to conform to a minimum weight limit (650 kg), have all-enveloping bodies with two seats and be fitted with lights. Obviously they are not sports-cars in the traditional sense and it is interesting to note that there are moves afoot to change the Championship regulations to outlaw these staggeringly-expensive devices and get back to something resembling more closely the original concept of sports-car racing.

## Saloon car racing

One of the most popular types of motor sport is saloon car racing. Here it is possible to see a wide variety of machinery ranging from the big American cars such as Ford Mustangs and Chevrolet Camaros right down to the tiny Minis and Hillman Imps. This type of racing is split into two main categories, that for basically standard, unmodified cars (Group 1), and that where considerable changes from the standard specification are allowed (Group 2). On the basis that a car costing £2,000 will probably be faster, irrespective of engine size, than one costing £1,000, the Group 1 cars are normally classified by price rather than by engine capacity. These unmodified cars with their soft springing are extremely spectacular to watch as they take the corners virtually on their door handles.

Most of the big international races for saloon cars and notably those for the European Touring Car Championship are held for the much-modified Group 2 cars. These cars can be fantastically expensive to build and a Ford Escort RS1600 in full Group 2 trim could set the proud owner back well over £6,000. Such a car would have an engine churning out over 275 bhp, a maximum speed of around 150 mph, a five-speed gearbox and racing tyres and suspension. In fact the car is an out-an-out racing car and is only really suitable for that purpose.

## Rallying

Next to racing the most widely practised form of motor sport is rallying. Rallies come in all shapes and sizes and range from one-night local affairs to the trans-global events such as the 1968 London-Sydney Marathon and the 1970 London-Mexico World Cup Rally, each of which involved distances in excess of 10,000 miles and lasted for nearly a month.

However, whether rallies last 24 hours or 24 days they all have one thing in common and that is that they are basically tests of regularity and reliability and not of

speed. Competitors have to complete the route in a specified time and penalties are incurred for being early as well as late. To make sure that a near-uniform average speed (usually 30 mph) is maintained throughout, control points are set up along the route at which each car must clock-in at a specified time. Again there are penalties for being early or late. Lateness at one control is not allowed to be made up by going flat out to the next!

Rallies are held on roads varying from main highways to unsurfaced tracks running through forests and mountains. In Sweden, a winter rally is held where part of the route is along a frozen river and artificial bends and corners are carved by snowploughs out of the deep snow covering the ice.

Many rallies have sections known as "special stages". These stages are on either private land or, in foreign countries, sections of public road closed to normal traffic. The average speeds set are very much higher than for the normal part of the route and can be as high as 70 mph for a rally such as the East African Safari. Most special stages are over dirt roads on which the top drivers often touch 100 mph or more.

It is, of course, the performances put up on the special stages which usually determine the winner. The average speeds set are such that it is extremely difficult to complete the stage on time and even the star drivers will lose time on most of these sections. In many rallies, though not all, it is possible to practice the stages beforehand and competitors take advantage of this to make notes which give them a detailed description of each section. Known as "pace notes" the descriptions include the nature of each corner, the length of the straights, the type of road surface and the speeds at which each part of the stage can be taken. Pace notes are written in a type of shorthand which can be easily read in a leaping, bouncing rally car and are called out to the driver by the navigator over an intercom system plugged into their crash helmets. The driver thus is given a complete word-picture of the road ahead which enables him to take blind bends at maximum speed in the knowledge that the corner is very much faster than it looks.

On a special-stage rally the navigator's function, in addition to calling the pace notes, is to drive the easy road sections and generally manage the operation. He is responsible for organising any service or repairs, making sure the car is on schedule and arranging for such things as food, maps and other details. The driver's job is mainly to drive the difficult road sections and the stages themselves.

However, many rallies, especially in the UK, do not have special stages and are exercises in pure navigation as well as driving. These are the one-night rallies of

Action at Oulton Park circuit.

about 200 miles in length where the route is kept secret until about half-an-hour before the start. The navigator is then given the route in the form of map references which he then has to work out and plot on his one-inch Ordnance Survey Maps. Distance between controls is often only a few miles and to remain on schedule needs extremely quick and accurate work on the part of the navigator as well as ability on the part of the driver.

Generally speaking rallies are for normal production saloon cars which, as with saloon-car racing, can be run under Group 1 rules (unmodified) or in the Group 2 category in which many changes to the standard specification are allowed. Naturally enough, modifications made to Group 2 rally cars are very different from those made to their racing sisters and are directed at making the suspension more suitable for rough roads and improving the general toughness of the car rather than concentrating on getting the maximum possible power from the engine. Needless to say Group 1 and Group 2 cars compete for separate awards in the same rally as well as against each other for outright victory. However, it is very rare to see a Group 1 car winning a rally outright for obvious reasons.

## Rally-cross

Closely linked with rallying is rally-cross. This comparatively recent development in motor sport had its origins in the idea that rally special stage laid out in the form of closed circuit would provide spectacular entertainment for spectators as well as providing good, inexpensive competition for the drivers. Rally-cross has rapidly grown in popularity in the UK and is now securing a strong foothold in Europe.

The average rally-cross circuit is about a mile in length and incorporates steep climbs and descents, sharp corners and includes a certain amount of tarmac as well as rough, cross-country-type going. Each race is usually a four-lap affair and involves four cars. The programme is arranged so that there are sufficient races to enable each competitor to compete against all the others. The winner is the driver who has the lowest aggregate time.

Rally-cross cars are usually super-tuned saloons for which all the interior trim and seats (except that for the driver) have been removed. Most popular subjects are Ford Escorts, Imps and Minis and all have had their

share of success. One or two "monsters" have also appeared including specially-factory-built, four-wheel-drive Ford Capris and BLMC Minis. Because of its spectacular nature, Rally-cross receives extensive television coverage and has been known to attract more TV viewers than even football.

## . . . and Autocross

Many people ask "what's the difference between Rally-cross and Auto-cross?" and it is true that there is a great deal of similarity between the two activities. However, Auto-cross is the older of the two having been "invented" as far back as 1947. A typical circuit will measure about half-a-mile and will be marked out in a big field by means of flags or inflatable plastic bollards. If drivers hit the course markers a penalty is added to their time and should they leave the circuit completely, they are disqualified.

A race or run will be of two or three laps duration and drivers are allowed several runs. The winner will usually be the driver who makes the fastest run, although sometimes the victor is determined on the basis of aggregate times as in Rally-Cross.

The cars used are basically the same as those employed for Rally-Cross though, unlike Rally-cross, one-off specials, owing nothing to any mass-production car, are also allowed. These specials are often most ingenious, some of them going so far as to have two engines, one driving the rear wheels, the other driving the front! Ford-engined Minis are not uncommon and a Porsche engine lurking beneath the skin of a Volkswagen Beetle is not unknown! Auto-cross is cheap, spectacular fun for competitors and spectators alike.

## Drag racing . . .

And now for something completely different! Drag racing has no parallel in motor sport and has one basic objective, to cover a quarter-mile for a standing start in the shortest time possible. Drag racing was born in the USA where it has a fantastic following, with drag strips all over the country. Only recently has it been imported to Britain where it is flourishing, though on a rather smaller scale. To say that the top competitors in this sport regularly cover 440 yards from a standing start in round about 6½ seconds probably does not mean very much. But imagine you are hurtling down a deserted aerodrome runway behind the wheel of a V-12 E-Type Jaguar at 140 mph. Standing on the runway ahead of you is the latest in American drag-racing machinery. As you draw level with the stationary monster it starts and you carry on at your breathtaking 140 per hour. Nearly 6½ seconds later and a quarter-of-a-mile further on there is a fantastic explosing of noise. The dragster has passed you doing about 230 mph and is still accelerating.

What kind of device is capable of this sort of performance? Well, for a start, it has a supercharged American V-8 engine of over 7 litres which runs on a mixture of nitromethane and alcohol. Net result is often around 1,500 bhp. There is no gearbox, only a clutch, and braking is mainly by one or more parachutes released immediately the car crosses the finish line. Engine, clutch housing and rear axle are bolted up as one unit and the driver usually sits directly above the axle casing. Stretching way ahead of the engine is a long tubular structure at the front of which are mounted the motor-cycle-type front wheels. No form of springing is provided. Known as "rails" these cars represent the ultimate in the art but one of the great attractions of drag-racing is the variety of way-out machinery that this branch of motor sport attracts. Jaguar engines in Ford Populars and Volkswagens full to the brim with

Chevrolet V-8's are just two of the many examples of the special-builders' virtuosity.

## Hill climbing

Whereas drag racing is one of the newest forms of motor-sport, Hill Climbing is one of the oldest. One of Britain's most famous hills, Shelsley Walsh in Worcestershire, has been in use since 1905 and so we may say that hill-climbing is as old as motor-sport itself. Hill-climbing is a race against the clock and the cars are despatched one at a time up the narrow, twisty and often very steep ascent. Because British law prohibits speed events on the public roads, the U.K. hills are all on private property and vary in length from just over 400 yards to one mile. However, in Europe no such restrictions exist and stretches of normal mountain road many miles in length are commonly employed. Naturally enough these roads are closed during an event!

In the British Isles the fastest cars on the hills are usually pukka racing cars such as the McLaren M10 Formula 5000 machine, though there are, of course, classes for all types of car including vintage and veteran models. In Europe the emphasis is on sports cars as well as pure racers but it is interesting to note that the fastest times on many of the hills have been achieved by Formula 2 cars.

Unfortunately in a single chapter such as this it is only possible to paint the broad outlines of a subject as vast as motor sport. Nevertheless one of the great things about motor-sport is that there is something in it for practically everyone. I hope there is something in it for you!

# TOMORROW'S CARS?

WITH FUEL AND engery crises recurring and suggestions of petrol rationing, the "car of tomorrow" has taken on a new image. Gone, perhaps, are the days of the Rolls Royce and the Aston Martin. Such cars suffer most from possible restriction on fuels.

Clearly, it will be the compact family saloon, like the economical Mini and the small-engined Fiat cars, which will be the major cars of tomorrow.

The initial problems of making a small car light yet strong enough to come up to future safety requirements are a headache for the designer. Make a small car heavy and fuel economy will suffer. Just about every manufacturer world wide must now be investigating new techniques of construction, new materials, and breaking with design traditions which have been practised (but admittedly constantly reviewed) for generations.

### "Cars for cities"

One major problem, especially in the crowded towns and cities of the United Kingdom, is the pure volume of traffic.

A decade ago, in 1964, a Government Committee was set up to investigate future trends in road vehicles. They were specifically concerned with their influence on city environments. "Cars for Cities", copies of which have probably been gathering dust on motoring editors' and designers' desks since publication in 1967 must now be finding an avid readership!

Two and four-seater "city cars" were suggested. Their lengths — about 6ft. 6in. and just under 8 feet respectively. The Mini, regarded by many a cramped four-seater, would seem palatial with her 10ft. 6in. length compared with a city car of only 8ft. in length!

Advantages? Well, for inter-city use, where the majority of private cars carry only one or two people, the concept is fine. Fuel economies would be good as a small engine only would be needed. Parking, too, would mean that three or four of these mini-minis could be parked in the space normally used by the average car of about 13 feet in length. This could be done by parking "nose-on" to the kerb.

More of these, the "mini-misers", could get on the road . . . but would we not eventually end up having just as much traffic chaos only with more individual vehicles vying for every foot of roadspace?

Various other solutions have been put forward — such as banning personal transport from city centres and forcing people to drive only to outskirts from where they could catch regular and frequent public service vehicles. Perhaps cities could impose special tolls on private vehicles entering their boundaries? Who knows what the situation could be in ten years time?

There have been several attempts to design the city car. Unfortunately, production tooling hasn't proved viable and many have been placed in mothballs.

# Tichy-TiCi

SOME DESIGNERS like Anthony Hill, have been brave enough to put their hard work and expertise where everyone else's mouth has been! With his first design of a city car, Anthony Hill produced a vehicle which was just over half the length of a BLMC Mini. She had a 500cc engine but never had a sniff of production possibility as there was not enough financial backing (or interest) at the time. Undaunted, Anthony Hill designed what he hoped would be a compromise which might just catch the imagination — TiCi, a city car which blended the excitement of a youthful "buggy" appeal with the attraction of being just 7ft. 5in. in length.

TiCi was first shown at the 1972 Racing Car Show and featured a glass reinforced plastic body shell with a similarly constructed floor pan moulding which was designed with integral seats for two. Made available in kit form, a purchaser had to add standard BLMC Mini bits to complete parts of the car not supplied. The engine, from a Mini too, also had to be fitted by the owner.

| | |
|---|---|
| Length | 89 inches |
| Width | 58 inches |
| Height | 47 inches |
| Weight | approx. 900lb. |
| Fuel Capacity | 6 gallons |
| Engine rating | 500cc |
| Seats | Two |
| Designer | Anthony Hill |

# The Comuta Car...

ONE MANUFACTURER prominent in design and research is the Ford Motor Company. As long ago as 1966, research staff were asked to investigate the feasibilities of producing a small, experimental electric car. Before the Government Committee published "Cars for Cities", Ford's baby electrically powered car had been christened Comuta.

Her design brief required that:
... she should be small enough to require minimum parking space.
... she should take up as little road space as possible when in use.
... should provide exceptional manoeuvrability for parking space access.
... should be quiet when under way
... be simple to drive.
... be inexpensive to buy and cheap to run
... and give off the minimum (if any) pollutants to the environment.

Despite the compact size of Comuta, the car had seating capacity for two adults and two children in an overal length of just 6ft. 8ins.

The main drawback of Comuta, and other similar experiments since, was to provide a fuel cell (or battery) which would provide enough "miles per amp hour". This problem is still receiving intensive investigation and research. In her original form, Comuta's two electric motors (each driving one of the rear wheels) had power enough to cover approximately 40 miles at a speed of 25 miles per hour. That was not her top speed — she had quite brisk acceleration for a vehicle of her type giving a figure of 0 to 30 miles per hour in less than 14 seconds, and could make 40 mph.

The batteries could, of course, be recharged — but if your journey was 41 miles and you had been travelling at 25½ miles per hour . . .

The rest of Comuta's equipment was almost "traditional". She had full lighting, direction indicators, windscreen wipers, washers and seat belts fitted. The dashboard had a "state of battery" indicator — the electric motor's fuel gauge.

Length . . . . . . . . 80 inches
Width . . . . . . . . 49.5 inches
Height . . . . . . . . 56 inches
Turning Circle . . 18 inches
Weight . . . . . . . . . 1200lb
Maximum speed . 40 mph
Acceleration to
  30 mph in . . . . . 13 secs.
Range . 40 miles at 25 mph

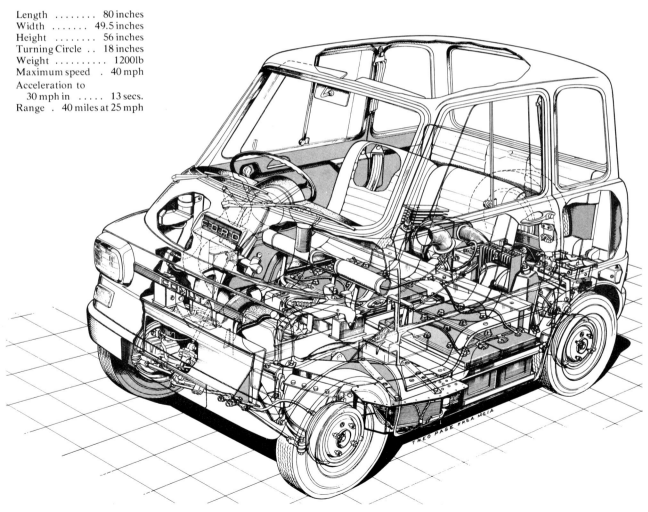

114

# MINISSIMA
... a town car based on the Mini

THE ORIGINAL Austin-Morris Minis set an unmatched standard of space-utilisation in 1959, with their transversely arranged engines and transmission units. Thus it was only logical that "Minissima" should be based on Mini running gear. This gave the maximum amount of passenger space within the overall length of 90 inches. This is 30 inches less than the already compact Mini, and allows parking at right angles to the kerb to save parking space.

Mechanically, the Minissima is a straightforward BLMC Mini 850 automatic, with minimal changes to adapt the chassis components to the shorter and more upright body design.

The front and rear subframes, with their respective suspension and braking systems are mounted so as to give a wheelbase of 59 inches (the wheelbase of a Mini saloon is about 80 inches). Using the standard rack and pinion steering, a turning circle of approximately 21 feet is possible.

The steering column is raked forward to suit the upright driving position. The body structure incorporates a Mini bulkhead panel in order to provide mounting points for the front subframe, steering rack and pedal pivot box.

Because of the rear-mounted door, the exhaust system is routed to a tailpipe which discharges to the offside in front of the rear wheel. The petrol tank is located under the front passenger seat, with the filler cap neatly concealed beneath a hinged section of the bodyside moulding. Space is also provided under the passenger

seat for a spare wheel. Perhaps in time British Leyland will fit a tyre such as the Dunlop Dunovo or Avon Safety Wheel which would mean that a spare need not be carried.

Inside the car, a Rover 2000-type instrument box is fitted flush with the broad facia panel, and the column stalks are of the type fitted to the Morris Marina and Austin Allegro models, controlling indicators, horn, headlamp dip and flash and wash/wipe.

Other controls are grouped on a horizontal panel to the right of the driver, and include the automatic gearbox selector lever, slide controls for the heater and choke, push buttons for lights and auxilaries, and a flap handle for the rear door release. This handle (an exterior door handle from a Morris Marina) is located by the driver as a child-proofing precaution, and operates the door latch via a Bowden cable. The handbrake lies behind the control panel.

When first shown at the 1973 Motor Show at Earls Court, Minissima was claimed to demonstrate an intelligent new concept in urban transport. Specifications are not fixed and alternative power units of up to 1300cc could be installed, and several aspects of the design would be modified to suit production requirements.

When the prototype was first shown, a large car hire company made serious approaches to British Leyland for the purchase of a large number of Minissimas — but not enough for BLMC to warrant setting up production facilities. And with the present talk of ever spiralling petrol costs, it would seem that an electrically-powered version (with a practical cruising speed) might arouse more interest.

## MINISIMA — DETAILS

| | |
|---|---|
| Length | 90 inches |
| Width | 59 inches |
| Height | 59 inches |
| Engine | 848cc (petrol) Automatic |
| B.H.P. | 38 b.h.p. |
| Designer | Bill Towns |

# See Motor Sport

Britain's racing circuits, hillclimbs and sprint courses.

# Racing Circuits

**AINTREE:** Aintree Automobile Racing Co. Ltd., Racecourse Offices, Liverpool 9.

Club racing; practice days organised by Aintree Circuit.

How to get there: Local bus services in frequent operation from central Liverpool.

**BISHOPSCOURT:** Bishopscourt Airfield, Bishopscourt, Downpatrick, Co. Down, N. Ireland.

Club racing.

How to get there: Bus service from Downpatrick to Ballyhornan passes circuit.

**BRANDS HATCH CIRCUIT,** Fawkham, Dartford, Kent.

International, National, Club and stock car racing; also occasionally karting.

How to get there: Bus — Greenline 719 from London to Wrotham. For local services telephone Swanley 2075. Train — from Victoria, Holborn Viaduct, Sevenoaks and south coast to Swanley. Special bus service from Swanley station for major meetings.

**CADWELL PARK:** Chas, Wilkinson, Cadwell Manor, Louth, Lincs.

International, National and Club racing for cars under 2000cc. Also stock cars, karting and televised rallycross.

How to get there: Bus — services from Lincoln and Sleaford to Horncastle. From Grimsby, Market Rasen and Lincoln to Louth.

**CASTLE COMBE CIRCUIT,** Chippenham, Wilts.

National and Club race meetings.

How to get there: Bus — 399 service from Bristol to Chippenham. Train — Chippenham station on Paddington to Bristol line.

**CROFT AUTODROME, CROFT,** Darlington, Co. Durham.

International and Club racing; also for non-television rallycross.

How to get there: Bus — service from Darlington station to circuit. Train — Darlington station from Kings Cross.

**CRYSTAL PALACE CIRCUIT,** Anerley Hill, London SE19.

International and Club racing; also occasional karting.

How to get there: Bus — 2, 2B, 3, 12, 49, 63A, 108, 122, 137, 154, 157, 227 services. Train — Southern Region trains to Crystal Palace, Penge East or Penge West.

**INGLISTON:** Scotcircuits Ltd., National Bank Chambers, Duns, Berwicks.

National and Club race meetings.

How to get there: Bus — regular service from Edinburgh. Train —Waverley station (Edinburgh) from Kings Cross.

**KIRKISTOWN CIRCUIT,** Kircubbin, Newtownards, Co. Down. (Apply to Secretary: 500 Motor Racing Club of Ireland).

National and Club race meetings.

How to get there: Bus from Newtownards to Portaferry via Cloughey passes about 1 mile from circuit.

**LLANDOW:** South Wales Automobile Club, 1-2 Wellington Street, Cardiff.

Club race meetings.

How to get there: Bus — service from Cowbridge to Llantwitmajor.

**LYDDEN:** William Mark Holdings Ltd., 71 West Street, Sittingbourne, Kent.

Club races, karting and televised rallycross; also occasional stock car meetings.

How to get there: Bus — East Kent Line Service 15 from Canterbury. Train — Shepherdswell on Southern Region Victoria to Dover.

**MALLORY PARK,** Kirkby Mallory, Leics.

International, National and Club racing.

How to get there: Bus — 688 service from Hinckley to Kirkby Mallory. 658 service from Leicester to Earl Shilton. Train — Leicester station. Timetable enquiries to Leicester 29811.

**OULTON PARK:** Cheshire Car Circuit Ltd., Oulton Park, Little Budworth, Tarporley, Cheshire.

International, National and Club racing.

How to get there: Bus — North Western Road Car Co. services from Manchester, Macclesfield, Warrington and Altrincham to Northwich, then shuttle service to circuit from bus station.

**RUFFORTH:** BRSCC, York House, 21 Park Street, Leeds 1.

Club racing.

How to get there: Bus — Local services from York. Train — York station, then by bus.

**SILVERSTONE CIRCUIT,** SILVERSTONE, Near Towcester, Northants, NN12 8TN.

International, National and Club racing.

How to get there: Bus — 345 service from Northampton bus station to Silverstone village. Train — Northampton station from Euston.

**SNETTERTON CIRCUIT,** Snetterton, Norwich, NOR 1OX.

International, National and Club racing. Occasional stock car racing.

How to get there: Bus — 12 service from Norwich to Attleborough. Train — Attleborough and Thetford stations on Norwich to Cambridge line.

**THRUXTON** (BARC), Thruxton Circuit, near Andover, Hants.

International, National and Club racing.

How to get there: Bus — Apply to Wilts & Dorset Motor Services Ltd., Bridge Street, Andover. Train — Southern Region stations to Andover.

# Hillclimb Courses

**BAITINGS DAM, YORKS**

Location: Blackstone Edge. 5 miles south-west of Sowerby.

Contact: N. J. Tudor Thomas, Lancashire Automobile Club, 10 Cannon Street, preston, Lancs.

**BARBON MANOR, WESTMORLAND.**

Location: 2¾ miles north-east of Kirkby Lonsdale.

Contact: R. Cannon, Westmorland Motor Club, Glenwood, Brigster, Nr. Kendall, Westmorland.

**BODIAM, SUSSEX**

Location: New House Farm, Bodiam.

Contact: A. G. Bird, East Sussex Car Club, Highview, Battery Hill, Fairlight, Hastings, Sussex.

**BRUNTON, HANTS.**

Location: North of Collingbourne, Kingston.

Contact: E. C. Britten, BARC (South West) Centre, 15 Bournemouth Road, Chandlers Ford, Hants, SO5 3DA.

**CADWELL PARK, LINCS.**

Location: 8 miles north-east of Horncastle.

Contact: J. K. Warrillow, BARC (East Midlands) Centre, 101 Station Road, Cropston, Leics.

**CASTLE HOWARD, YORKS.**

Location: 5 miles west of Malton.

Contact: P. Croft, Yorkshire, Sports Car Club, 56 Reins Road, Rastrick, Brighouse, Yorks.

**CRAIGANTLET, CO. DOWN.**

Location: 8 miles east of Belfast.

Contact: W. Kinnear, Ulster Automobile Club, 3 Botanic Avenue, Belfast, BT7 1JG.

**DITCHAM HILL, SUSSEX.**

Location: 3 miles east of Petersfield.

Contact: Miss J. Dutton, Chichester Motor Club, 75 St. Leodegars Way, Hunston, Chichester.

**DOUNE, PERTHSHIRE**

Location: 1¼ miles west of Doune.

Contact: Competition Secretary, Lothian Car Club, Scotia Office Machines, 2/4 Castle Terrace, Edinburgh 1.

**FINTRAY HOUSE, ABERDEENSHIRE**

Location: 8½ miles north-west of Aberdeen.

Contact: Competition Secretary, Aberdeen and District Motor Club, 12 Golden Square, Aberdeen.

**GT. AUCLUM, BERKS**

Location: 6 miles south-west of Reading.

Contact: D. Hogg, Hants and Berks Motor Club, 22 Broadlands Court, Wokingham Road, Bracknell, Berks.

**GURSTON DOWN, WILTS**

Location: 1 mile west of Broadchalke.

Contact: M. Norris Hill, BARC (South West) Centre, Wentways, Beauworth, Airesford, Hants.

**HAREWOOD, YORKS.**

Location: Stockton Farm, 7½ miles north-east of Leeds.

Contact: M. S. Wilson, BARC (Yorkshire) Centre, Silver Royd House, Leeds, LS12 4QQ.

**HEMERDON HILL, DEVON**

Location: 2½ miles north-east of Plympton.

Contact: Competition Secretary, Plymouth Motor Club, Raynham Court, Raynham Road, Penlee, Plymouth.

**LOTON PARK, SALOP**

Location: 8½ miles west of Shrewsbury.

Contact: John H. Dorsett, Hagley and District Light Car Club, Alpha Business Services, Mart Lane, Stourport-on-Severn, Worcs.

**ODDICOMBE, DEVON**

Location: North-west of Torquay.

Contact: J. Burgoyne, Torbay Motor Club, Green Pastures, Veille Lane, Shiphay, Torquay.

**OLIVERS MOUNT, YORKS.**

Location: 1 mile south of Scarborough via A64.

Contact: M. S. Wilson, BARC (Yorkshire) Centre, Silver Royd House, Leeds, LS12 4QQ.

**PONTYPOOL, SOUTH WALES**

Location: Pontypool Park, Glamorgan.

Contact: N. Jones, BARC (South Wales) Centre, 5 Holywell Road East, Abergaveny, Mons.

**PRESCOTT, GLOS.**

Location: 5 miles north-east of Cheltenham

Contact: Godfrey Eaton, Bugatti Owners Club, 40 Bartholomew Street, Newbury, Berks.

**SCAMMONDEN, YORKS**

Location: Scammonden Dam, 5 miles west of Huddersfield.

Contact: M. S. Wilson, BARC (Yorkshire) Centre, Silver-Royd House, Leeds, LS12 4QQ.

**SHELSLEY WALSH, WORCS.**

Location: 10 miles west of Worcester via B4204.

Contact: G. Flewitt, Midland Automobile Club, 4 Vicarage road, Edgbaston, Birmingham, B15 3ES.

# Sprint Courses

**AINSDALE BEACH, LANCS**

Location: Ainsdale, Nr. Southport.

Length of course: 1 mile.

Contact: David Aukland, Liverpool Motor Club, 6 Hard Land, St. Helens, Lancs.

**BLACKBUSHE, HANTS**

Location: 2 miles west of Blackwater; approach by A30 from Bagshot.

Length of course: 1,200 yards.

Contact: P. D. Cunnell, BARC (Surrey) Centre, Overdrift, Tower Hill, Dorking, Surrey.

**BURTONWOOD, LANCS**

Location: Airfield, 2 miles north-west of Warrington.

Length of course: 1.7 miles.

Contact: K. Anson, Chester Motor Club, 33 Coniston Drive, Frodsham, Via Warrington, Cheshire.

**CURBOROUGH, STAFFS**
Location: 2½ miles north-east of Lichfield on unclassified road from A38.
    Length of course: 900 yards.
    Contact: M. Finnemore, Shenstone and District Car Club, 3 High Street, Sutton Coldfield, Warwicks.

**DUXFORD, CAMBS.**
Location: 7 miles north of Royston.
    Length of course: 1,400 yards.
    Contact: A. J. Scamber, Cambridge Car Club, 26 High Street, Dry Drayton, Cambridge.

**GREENHAM COMMON, BERKS.**
Location: 2 miles south-east of Newbury.
    Length of course: 1 mile.
    Contact: T. Hellier, Southsea Motor Club, 21 Goodwood Close, Cowplain, Hants.

**MILFIELD, ROXBURGH**
Location: 6 miles north-west of Wooler.
    Length of course: 440 yards.
    Contact: D. G. Campbell, Hawick and Border Car and Motor Cycle Club, Wilderburn, Galashiels, Selkirk.

**CRIMOND, ABERDEEN**
Location: 8 miles south-east of Fraserburgh.
    Length of course: 1.4 miles.
    Contact: I. A. Hay, Aberdeen and District Motor Club, 12 Golden Square, Aberdeen, Scotland.

**MORETON-IN-THE-MARSH, GLOS.**
Location: 4 miles north of Stow-on-the-Wold, approach via Fosse Way.
    Length of course: 1,350 yards.
    Contact: A. Lapsley, North Cotswold Motor Club, Fujima, Swan Close, Moreton-in-the-Marsh, Glos.

**NORTH WEALD, ESSEX**
Location: 4 miles north-east of Epping.
    Length of course: 440 yards.
    Contact: D. Crome, Harrow Car Club, 66 Sherington Avenue, Pinner, HA8 0LT.

**PRINCES WAY, BLACKPOOL.**
Location: Part of the promenade at North Shore, Blackpool.
    Length of course: 1,000 yards.
    Contact: M. Davis, Longton and District Motor Club, 38 Pope Lane, Penwortham, Preston, Lancs.

**SANTA POD, NORTHANTS**
Location: 6 miles south-west of Wellingborough.
    Length of course: 440 yards.
    Contact: 95/97 Martins Road, Shortlands, Bromley, Kent.

**ST. EVAL, CORNWALL.**
Location: 4 miles north-west of St. Colomb Major.
    Length of course: 1½ miles.
    Contact: B. Lanyon, Newquay Motor Club, 29 Polsue Way, Tresillian, Truro, Cornwall.

**WOODVALE, LANCS.**
Location: 5 miles south of Southport.
    Length of course: 2.6 miles.
    Contact: A. Iddon, Lancashire Automobile Club, 7 Lyndon Avenue, Great Harwood, Blackburn, Lancs.

**YEOVILTON, SOMERSET**
Location: 5 miles north of Yeovil.
    Length of course: 870 yards.
    Contact: A. Mansfield, Yeovil Car Club, 2 Summerfield Park Avenue, Ilminster, Somerset.

# Useful Names and Addresses

**British Automobile Club (BARC),**
*Sutherland House, 5/6 Agrgyll Street,*
*London W1.*

**British Drag Racing and Hot Rod Association,**
*Mrs. E. Bartlett, 55 West End Court,*
*West End Lane, Stoke Poges, Bucks.*

**British Jalopy Racing Association,**
*G. Edmond, 16 Claremount Road,*
*Gloucester.*

**British Racing and Sports Car Club (BRSCC),**
*Empire House, Chiswick High Road,*
*London W4.*

**British Stock Car Racing Association,**
*232 High Road, Wood Green,*
*London N22.*

**British Trial and Rally Drivers Association,**
*D. B. Smith, Hurst Street,*
*Reddish, Stockport, Cheshire.*

**Car Grasstrack Racing Organisation,**
*P. Beaumont, 53 Meadowfield, Sleaford,*
*Lincolnshire.*

**Federation Internationale de l'Automobile (FIA) and Commission Sportive Internationale (CSI),**
*8 Place de la Concorde, Paris.*

**Formula Ford International,**
*N. Brittan, 35 Alwyne Road,*
*London N1.*

**Formula Vee Association,**
*Volkswagen House, Brighton Road,*
*Purley, Surrey CR2 2UQ.*

**Jim Russell International Racing Drivers School,**
*Snetterton Circuit, Norwich NOR 10X and at Mallory Park*
*Circuit, Kirby Mallory, Leicester (Earl Shilton 2841).*

**Mini Seven Club,**
*M. Burton, 'Moonrakers', Great Coxwell,*
*Near Faringdon, Berkshire.*

**Motor Circuit Developments Limited,**
*Brands Hatch, Fawkham, Near Dartford,*
*Kent.*

**Motor Racing Stables Limited,**
*Brands Hatch, Fawkham, Near Dartford, Kent, and at Silverstone*
*Circuit, Siverstone Near Towcester, Northants.*

**Northern Car Track Racing Organisation,**
*E. Ganderton, 114 The Garland,*
*Clifton, York.*

**Royal Automobile Club (Motor Sport Divison),**
*31 Belgrave Square,*
*London SW1*

**750 Motor Club,**
*D. Bradley, 'Zolder', 16 Woodstock Road,*
*Witney, Oxfordshire.*

**Thruxton Saloon Car Racing School,**
*Thruxton Circuit, Near Andover,*
*Hants.*

**Vintage Sports Car Club (VSCC),**
*Bone Lane, (off Mill Lane),*
*Newbury, Lancs.*
*Newbury, Berks.*

# INDEX